L

IS

YOURS

from heartbreak to heart awake

ABIGAIL YARDIMCI

Britain's Next
BESTSELLER

Cover design by Abigail Yardımcı/Miacello
ISBN: 978-1-906954-505
Printed in the U.K

In memory and celebration of my brilliant Dad

'An awake heart is like a sky that pours light.'
Håfez

CONTENTS

HOW THIS BOOK WORKS_

In 2006 I had the most unexpected, tumultuous and life-altering year.

I'll never forget it. And that's why I wrote about it in three parts, of which this book, 'Life Is Yours' is the first.

I decided to capture the year through the eyes of a fictitious character primarily because when I was a kid I obsessed over the name 'Jess' and couldn't understand why my parents hadn't seen fit to give me it, when it was clearly the most glamorous name ever.

But also, because I needed to create a bit of distance between me and the story. A gap where I could understand more deeply what had happened and allow the juicy stuff to really come to light. It meant I could have a bit of artistic license with the order of events, I could merge characters where there were too many to keep track of, and change names out of respect for people who might recognise themselves in the pages.

I hope you enjoy the story because the majority of it happened exactly like that, with incredible people showing up and blowing my mind with their timing, their authenticity and their undeniable part in helping my heart finally wake up. The rest of it is yummy fiction that I hope you relish in your own way.

And now – Turkey…

FINDING THE FIRE_

AND SO SHE kept on walking.

Regardless of her mother's voice calling helplessly against the night wind. It was growing fainter and fainter with every step. And so she kept on walking.

The beach was cool and calm. The moon cast a stream of white light which she followed through silent tears. She wiped her hair off her cheeks and concentrated on sinking her bare feet deep into the sand. She carried on like this for a while. Moon, feet, hair, tears. Moon, feet, hair, tears. Until - dredging it up from god knows where - she took a deep breath and stopped.

What the hell am I doing here? Lindy felt like screaming it. Somebody might hear and actually give her a decent answer. But the moon and the sea and the night gazed back at her with the nothingness she'd grown accustomed to.

She asked herself again, *what the hell am I doing here?* She repeated it like a mantra in her head until it was interrupted by the memory of her mother's pleading voice the day it had all happened. "Come on now duck. You must have known something was wrong. All the signs were there." *What a thing to say,* Lindy thought. As far as she was concerned there had been no signs at all. Nothing. No way she could have known what would happen.

She looked back in the direction of the apartment block and saw that the lights in her parents' apartment had been switched off. *They've gone out then,* she thought. *So much for New Year not being complete without their only daughter.* A well-timed comment from her dad about a nice cold glass of beer and a double-helping of sodding baklava, would have been enough for her mother to snatch up her handbag and stalk off down to the restaurant complex like Holidaymaker of the Bloody Year.

Sighing from the pit of her stomach she asked herself yet again why she'd come on holiday with her parents. On the surface things weren't bad. She was young; fit and well; in a half-decent job; in a half-decent flat. But it was New Year's Eve, 2006 was about to turn into 2007, and she hadn't even scraped the surface of all the useful things she should have done by now. And here she was standing alone on a cold, deserted beach in the South of Turkey with no obvious path towards any of those useful things. Shoulders hunched in a thick woolly jumper she'd had since she was a teen, legs shivering and white-knuckled hands grasping her dangling trainers by the laces. Her mum and dad had done a bunk and she was properly alone. Alone at a time when you are supposed to be with people. Alone at a time when you are supposed to be tipping back all manner of drinks, talking about all manner of things, and making all manner of plans for your bright and promising future.

She started to walk again. As she walked further along the beach and into the calm of the night, the lights behind her grew dimmer and the image she had of her parents sitting smugly together slowly faded.

Lindy knew really that her foul mood had nothing to do

with them. She knew that their offer to take her on holiday was dragged out of a love they didn't know how else to express. But how was she supposed to get out of this one herself? She wanted to make things better but was petrified of coming out of this world where you could cry and scream and rant and nobody expected you to be normal. At least, not yet.

It was then that she looked up and saw a deep orange glow close to the shore. There was a tiny fire burning in a rocky alcove up ahead and it carried the scent of charred wood across the beach to where she stood. It looked like somebody had got it going and then abandoned it, probably in favour of a good night out. She looked around and, because the beach was empty apart from a few couples off in the distance, she decided that the fire definitely did not belong to anybody anymore and therefore she could sneak in and claim it.

She reached the alcove, sat down and breathed in the heady smell of the charcoal. She found a stick to poke the fire with (because that's what you did with fires, you poked them with a stick), and for the first time that evening, Lindy took in her surroundings. Sea lapping, stars twinkling, breeze blowing, fire burning and the dark sky blanketing her softly.

Staring into the fire, she slipped into a delicious numbness. Her breathing evened out and her tears dried to a glaze on her cheeks. In her mind she saw one of those sliding plastic puzzles she used to get for Christmas as a child. All the pieces were definitely there, but they were always arranged in the wrong order so the picture never made any sense. Every time this meant the pieces had to be pulled apart and mixed up again, ready for the next attempt.

Suddenly the orange flames jumped and sparks flew

sharply across the sand. Lindy snapped out of her trance and looked up to see the dark silhouette of somebody standing over her. And they had just thrown some wood onto the fire. That somebody crouched down, edging into the light of the fire and smiled, her rounded face already glowing.

"So you found my fire? I wondered if somebody would."

"GOD, I'm sorry – I thought it'd been, y'know, abandoned or something."

Lindy stood up and backed away from the fire. The woman sat down on the sand, stretched out her legs and flapped her feet like a happy toddler. She smiled at Lindy across the glowing embers.

"It's fine really. I'm happy to share it if you want. My name's Jess."

The thought of heading back in the direction of the holiday complex made Lindy feel sick and she'd just been getting used to taking refuge in the beach. Maybe it wouldn't be so bad to spend some time in the company of a complete stranger. Somebody who knew nothing about the horrific mess she was in the middle of. So Lindy sat back down directly opposite Jess. "Thanks. I'll just stay for a bit if that's okay. Oh, and I'm Lindy."

"Great." Jess said.

She gave Lindy a friendly smile for a few seconds and then looked out to the dark sea. Lindy stole a quick look at her new companion. She was tall and slim with her long legs now folded up beneath her and her hands rested casually on her knees. Her hair hung in loose, blonde curls down to her shoulders, the light from the fire revealing some rich copper tones. She wore a purple hoodie which was far too big for her, with frayed edges on the cuffs and neckline and it reminded Lindy of something like a comfort blanket. Her jeans were well-worn, turned up at the bottom to show sandaled feet.

In basic terms Jess was tall, straight and plain, but there was something more to her that brought to mind a softness, a strange kind of grace.

As Jess turned to warm her hands she gazed into the fire as if she was sharing a secret with it. Lindy kept watching. She watched as Jess's blue grey stare softened slowly and melted into the flames of the fire.

After a while Jess blinked and sat back. She buried her hands into the sand and shuffled her legs out again.

"So, I suppose in a few hours, we'll all be raising our glasses and toasting our future."

"Yeah. I suppose." Lindy had almost forgotten what night it was.

"It's funny, isn't it? I mean, that we never think to do that on a normal day. Why do we all have to do it at the same time on the same night in the same pissed-up way?" Jess threw her hands in the air and talked to the sky. "What if it's not the right time for some people? What if yesterday was a better time to do it? Or tomorrow? Or next year?

"Or what if we don't want to do it at all?"

"Well exactly. What if we don't want to do it at all?" Jess laughed and looked right at Lindy. The warmth of her look was a bit startling, so much so that Lindy realised she was holding her breath. When Jess looked away, she exhaled quietly. Jess continued, "So we must have both thought the beach was a better place to be. Calmer, cooler, quieter . . ."

"Easier."

"Yes, easier."

"Nicer, simpler, unable to fuck you over."

Jess laughed loudly and threw her hands in the air. "Okay, I'll go with that! You can make a friend out of anything so why not a beach?"

Lindy noticed something silver glinting from underneath the cuff of Jess's jumper. It was a chunky bracelet made up of glossy silver spheres and a twisted rope chain. She had a matching necklace too which she now twisted and turned between her thumb and forefinger. Lindy almost tutted over the fashion crime of teaming something so beautiful with jeans and a jumper, but had to admit they suited Jess regardless.

Lindy wondered what the fuck was going on here. She would usually run a mile from random women who built fires in isolated spots on Turkish beaches, openly inviting strangers to join them. Not to mention all the time spent looking skywards and laughing like a lunatic. But there was something about Jess that was grudgingly intriguing.

She may as well give in to her curiosity. "So what brings you here on New Year's Eve then, Jess?"

"Hah! Now that's a good question. I could ask you the same but I'm sure you'll tell me if you want to."

Jess added some more wood to the fire and pulled her jumper up around her ears, leaving an inviting silence. For a second Lindy was tempted to spit it all out. Tell Jess about the whole damn thing from start to finish. But the words just wouldn't surface and the sentences so over-used anyway they seemed pathetic.

After a while Jess said, "Well, you wouldn't believe me if I told you."

"Maybe I would."

Jess laughed again. This time slower and deeper. "What brings me to this beach on New Year's Eve?" She trailed her fingers in the sand for a few seconds, making grooves around the fire. Lindy leaned back into the cool, flat rock of the alcove and got ready to listen.

Jess looked up at her. "Okay, I'll tell you."

JACK & JESS_

New Year's Eve 2005.

I'm in my most favourite scruffy pub with a couple of best mates and my boyfriend. No, not my boyfriend. My fiancée. Jack.

We've come to see a band that we fancy booking for our wedding. We have no clue when our wedding is going to be, and this is pretty much the first step we've taken (aside from actually getting engaged) to make any kind of plans for it. And we're having a blast. We're dancing and joking and laughing about the thought of our parents trying to dance to this weird, Yiddish-like, jazz-funk hybrid. The pot-bellied, clumsy-footed image is just too much and we laugh till it hurts. Life feels good and next year is looking great.

Jack and I met at university on a creative arts course. He was an actor and I was all about theatre design so we'd both signed up to be in a cringingly pretentious theatre piece in order to pass the final unit of our degrees. After months of over-exerted flirtations and ridiculously lust-fuelled comments, we finally got together. God, it was amazing. I was smitten by his sharp sense of humour, naughty brown eyes and dark, stocky sexiness. Like any couple in the throes of early romance, we moulded ourselves around each other in a borderline obsessive way. He told me he loved me after four days and I felt like all my Christmases had come at once. But, having always been Little Miss Sensible, I stated that it was ridiculous to claim to be in love after a measly four days and that we needed more time to get to know each other. And so we had that time. Loads of it. And within a few months I was well and truly loved up.

After university we rented a tiny excuse-of-a-house on a well dodgy estate near my north-eastern hometown. Jack made a big step by moving away from his folks down south, which made me realise just how serious he was about making this thing work. In our new house, damp was like a nagging flatmate, the windows were smothered in rotten eggs thrown by local kids, and the roof was about to cave in. But we didn't care. It was ours and that was all that mattered.

Our first couple of years together were by no means smooth. Jack and I – it seemed – were very different people. Me – methodical, thoughtful, sensitive and organised to the point of folding my knickers into little colour-co-ordinated triangles. Him – passionate, exuberant, intense and spontaneous to the point of going out for a pint of milk and coming back three days later with a gang of new mates and a missing tooth. We had so many fiery moments and definitely knew how to push each other's buttons. And we made a steady habit out of it.

But I kept telling myself that this was healthy. Your soul mate is supposed to push your buttons. How else do you learn about yourself? And anyway, he'd given up so much to be with me. Not many people would volunteer to shack up in a freezing cold climate with rowdy northerners, and I felt I owed it to him to be more understanding, more accommodating. So I was. And I tried every day to be more so.

After Jack had been through a few nightmarish jobs and me working for a stuffy local authority, we decided we had to do something 'arty' again. And if we couldn't find the right job in the papers then we would damn well start our own business. We recognised that those egg-slinging kids weren't really that bad and were actually just intensely bored. So we started coming up with ideas to give them something positive to do. Like acting, dancing, painting, sculpting and writing. After a few small projects we worked out that the chance to be creative tends to give young people – or anybody for that matter – the courage to finally be themselves. Or, to coin a phrase we'd learned at university, 'to find the fire that burned in their bellies'. So, after a few projects, we decided to call the business 'Firebelly'.

And Firebelly evolved because Jack and I were a damn good team. We'd never worked so hard in our lives . . . and it started to pay off because within one year we were able to leave our jobs and work for ourselves full time.

We were on a roll. We invited some uni mates to join in and help us develop the business. We stayed awake till three in the morning, whispering in bed about all the wonderful projects we could do. If we went out, the conversation always turned to Firebelly and what we could do with it next.

I even managed to relax about Jack making such a big life change because he started to attract his own friends and find his own strengths. By becoming less dependant on each other we fell in love all over again and rediscovered all the things about each other we'd almost forgotten. We worked hard and we played hard and we loved life.

After four years, Jack asked me to marry him. It was totally unexpected because we'd talked about marriage loads of times before and had always brushed it off as not important at all. We were quite happy living in sin thank you very much. But then one day, whilst scoffing some Cantonese food, he just bloody well asked me. I took in his nervous smile and the pause in his breath and I knew, without a shadow of a doubt, that I wanted to grow old with this man. So I said yes. Yes, of course I'll marry you.

And so it continued. Life together was everything I ever imagined a good relationship to be: challenging, loving, protective, humorous, surprising. After a little while we started talking about what our wedding would be like; when we'd have children and how we'd bring them up; what kind of home we'd have and where it would be. We made all our plans together and took pride in snatching glimpses of the future.

Before we knew it, we'd been together for over seven years. Seven years. In that time we'd set up a business together; been through several homes, cars, loans, holidays, friends, arguments, problems and discoveries. Our families (the living epitome of the North / South divide) could finally tolerate each other; we had a cute little cross-collie dog called Dinah, real plans to get married and had just bought our first gorgeous little cottagey-type-house. It felt like life was laid out for us on a plate.

Jess and Jack. Jack and Jess.

So back to the scruffy pub and the bizarre Yiddish jazz music. We stumble outside for some fresh air and sit on one of the rickety beer garden tables, shivering and nudging closer to each other. I can see out over the city valley below the pub and keep thinking how beautiful all the orange pin-prick lights are against the utter blackness of the December sky. I turn into Jack's broad chest and wait for his arms to pull me in. But they don't. In fact his body hasn't softened at all. He is stiff and upright.

I pull back and look right at him. He is looking square ahead and his brow is set in a stiff, dark frown. I am beginning to wonder where the Jack from two minutes ago has gone and rack my brains to think of something someone could have done to upset him during the short journey from inside the pub to the beer garden.

With what seems like all the effort in the world he turns his head and he looks at me hard. I've never seen so much pain in a person's eyes. And a sense of dread starts creeping up from my toes to my heart. Before I know what I'm saying the words just tumble out of my mouth: "do you love me?"

He looks at me and looks at me and looks at me. He hasn't said anything yet but already I can feel the tears prickling my eyes. Sharp. Hot. Full.

He looks at me. "Jess . . . I don't know if I love you."

GOING HOME_

AT FIRST HIS answer doesn't mean anything to me.

It is alien. Absurd.

But then it works its way into the present moment. And it stings. It slaps. It pounds.

"I'm sorry Jess. I know now's not a good time, but I couldn't stand it another minute. I just don't know what's going on in my head . . . " And he goes off into a speech that I can't listen to. I'm nodding my head, trying to be attentive, but really it is all I can do to stop myself from bursting into hysterical banshee mode.

He doesn't know if he loves me. He doesn't know if he loves me. He doesn't know if he loves me.

He mumbles something about getting a taxi home and disappears into the sickening glow of the pub. I am distantly aware that my mouth is agape and if I don't close it soon there will be a drastic dribble situation. I clamp shut my jaw, stiffen my shoulders and get up to walk to the end of the deserted street, my flat footsteps providing a dull, rhythmical soundtrack to this horror. I want the blackness of the night to scoop me up and send me off to some other world, one where I don't have to deal with what's going on. Whatever the hell that actually is.

Finally Jack appears from nowhere and joins me under a stark white streetlamp where millions of white dewdrops are falling slowly, slowly to the shiny concrete pavement. We stand a thousand miles apart. I am sniffling, shaking my head, staring into space. He is tense, pale, shuffling his feet. While we're waiting for the taxi, we can hear the excruciatingly jolly evening in the pub carry on. And, inevitably, amongst laughs, whistles, shouts and cheers, it comes. The countdown from ten to one; from last year to this year; from old life to new life; from love to loss.

In the taxi I let him do the small talk with the driver and I sink into the back seat with my eyes closed and mascara-black tears streaking down my face. I'm giving myself a mental pep-talk. Stay calm, don't assume the worst, he's just confused, it'll be okay.

Back home we sit on the sofa like a couple of sick strangers in a doctor's waiting room. The room is hauntingly still. Finally I ask him some questions because it feels like that's what I should be doing. "How long have you been feeling like this? Have I done something wrong? What do we do now?" And of course the million dollar question, "Is there somebody else?"

He does a good job of not answering any of the questions fully but lingers in their territory. He's only been having these feelings for a couple of weeks. He doesn't know where they've come from. He feels like he's living somebody else's life. At this point I have to butt in. "Jack, if you don't love me anymore then you have to tell me so we can split up. I need to know."

"For fuck's sake. Nobody said anything about splitting up. Don't put words in my mouth Jess."

Now if there's one thing I can't bear, it's not knowing where I stand. I don't do limbo land. So into the hours of the early morning, when the only people who should be awake are partygoers, our crying turns into shouting, shouting turns into screaming and, finally, screaming turns into a long, cold silence. A silence that tells us it's time to go to bed. Without either of us saying a word he sets up camp on the sofa (which is a first in our whole seven years) and I take the bedroom.

This night is absolutely the longest I've ever had. The absence of his body fills the bed so much I think that it might be possible to get lost in it. The man I have loved and known over the years has suddenly become the biggest stranger in the release of one single comment on one single night.

I don't sleep. Of course I don't sleep. Instead I toss, turn, sit, stand, curl-up, stretch out, but eventually just watch the agonisingly slow hands of the clock on the bedroom wall until they draw to seven o'clock. The time when I know my parents will be getting up to walk their dogs.

I get up. I dress in a ridiculous pyjama top and baggy jeans combo and creep out of the bedroom. I take one long look at him sleeping on the sofa and feel an urge to cuddle into him, slip back into his heart like a princess in a fairy tale. But this is no fairy tale. And I need to get out of this house.

I say goodbye to our dog Dinah, who I leave as some sort of company for Jack and I leave him a short note.

Gone to mam and dad's. We both need some time to think. Call me later.

And then I close the door, get in the car, and drive away.

OFFICIAL SEPARATION_

FIFTEEN MINUTES of trance-like driving brings me to a halt in my parents' driveway.

My mam is outside the house, chucking a load of recycling into the wheelie bin. I get out of the car and fling myself at her. A new wave of tears gushes out. Without a word she flips the lid on the bin and steers me inside.

Without a word.

The morning passes unwillingly. Tissues. Cups of tea. Whispers. A pattern emerges of my parents taking turns to sit with me while the other one gets on with their usual routine. They try to offer encouragement and practical advice, and my mam even suggests that: "perhaps you should be happy with seven years with a nice man – not many people even get that far!". I am torn between gratitude and exasperation at this comment, but remind myself that anything is better than sitting at home waiting for Jack to wake up.

My parents go out for the day so I sit in my dad's old,

spongy armchair and stare at a muted television, hoping that the silent images will encourage sleep. When I realise that sleep is a physical impossibility, I pick up the phone and try to get in touch with some of my friends. Of course no-one answers. It is New Year's Day after all, and most of them are probably lying in bed, nurturing a hangover, scoffing festive food or all of the above.

At times my mind feels gloriously empty and I am not thinking about anything. If I stare at the television for long enough, all the pictures merge into a dance of blotted colour and I can just zone out, switch off, extract. But it only ever lasts for seconds before reality punches me hard and forces me to remember last night, hearing Jack's words clearly, "I don't know if I love you."

When my mobile phone rings I nearly jump out of my skin. Bloody hell, it's Jack. I look around as if I'll find someone else to answer it but I'm alone on this one. "Hello?"

"Hi Jess. . . are you okay?"

I manage a kind of burble and will myself to regain the power of speech. Then I hear him sigh and realise that his breath is shaking.

"Jess, I need to do some thinking. And I think it's best if I leave the house, you know? Go somewhere else?"

"Absolutely."

"I've spoken to Betsy and Ikram and I'm going to go and stay with them for a while in town."

"Okay. A while?"

"Yeah. I think we need some time apart. Maybe . . . a week?"

And that was that. Decided. An official separation.

The rest of the phone call just plays itself out and the next thing I know I am left standing in the middle of my parents' living room, one half of a potentially failed relationship, alone, unwanted, discarded.

Fuck.

THE WEEK FROM HELL_

AND SO BEGAN the week From Hell.

Eventually on New Year's Day I managed to get hold of my best friend, Gillie. She'd been with Jack and I the night before and witnessed the whole dancing, laughing, happiest-couple-in-the-world thing and couldn't believe it when I told her what had happened: "Shit. Is this the same Jack we're talking about? Jack with the never-ending crush on you? Shit". She came straight to the rescue with soup (which I couldn't eat), movies (which I couldn't watch) and words of wisdom (which, of course, I couldn't listen to).

Gillie and I had been friends since our first day at university when she'd joined me all sleepy-eyed in the breakfast queue. I remember standing there with her, in the massive queue that snaked out into the freezing cold misty morning. We stamped our feet and jiggled up and down to keep warm. She bumped me gently with her elbow and smiled. "Hmmm, bacon." She'd drooled.

"Hmmm, toast." I'd added.

"With Marmite." She licked her lips.

"Are you joking? With peanut butter!" And that was it. A list of breakfast items sparked up a friendship neither of us knew would still be going strong ten years later.

Gillie's easy-going character was personified in her appearance. Playful, jewel green eyes, ridiculously long, swishy brown hair, soft curvy figure and hippy-chick clothes. We quickly found out we shared a naughty sense of humour and a passion for the arts. We lived on the same floor in halls of residence and by the third year of university we were housemates / sisters / joined at the hip. We shared everything: art materials, books, wine, clothes, money and food and after university, Gillie also moved to the North East to help Jack and I set up Firebelly. After years of living and working together, I'd seen Gillie change and mature. Her hippyish streak had morphed into a real devotion to fashion that would terrify anybody's bank balance and her hair shorter, redder, but still just as impressive. Put it this way, that girl was no stranger to turning heads pretty much wherever she went.

During the Week From Hell, Gillie became my pair of crutches. She showed me how to put one foot in front of the other and led me everywhere I needed to go. Without Jack or I managing to go to work, Gillie went to the office every day and made sure that the very basic operations of Firebelly were ticking over. Then she dedicated all other time to me me me.

When Gillie thoughtfully rallied round some of my other friends, I certainly wasn't going to win any prizes for my social skills. I couldn't look anybody straight in the eye. Out of shame or embarrassment or what I don't know, but I managed to develop an outstanding skill of staring at the floor and shaking my head in apparent disbelief. I didn't eat. I didn't sleep. I didn't smile. I didn't do anything apart from throw up, avoid people's eyes and think about Jack.

Most of my mates thought that Jack would come round in the end. This was the famous Jack and Jess, wasn't it? The Jack and Jess who'd built a successful company off the back of chavvy kids chucking eggs at their house. I wanted to believe them but knew this was dangerous ground. Based on my seven years of knowing Jack, I knew it wasn't a matter of coming round. It was a matter of dealing with a doubt neither of us had ever had before. Of course we'd had hard times – what couple doesn't? But hadn't we always had that underlying, solid bedrock of love? Where the hell was that when we needed it?

On top of it all, we were about to recruit a new artist at work. It was the first time we'd ever gone down the path of formal recruitment, and had been naturally nervous about inviting a stranger to share in our precious company. And I, in my colour-coded, knicker-folding glory, had originally demanded that the successful candidate be nothing short of perfect. But now my life seemed to be falling apart, I didn't give a flying shit if we recruited the Loch Ness Monster. Oh, and the job interviews were scheduled right in the middle of my Week From Hell. Perfect.

So Gillie took charge and mercifully arranged for the chair of our board to attend the interviews instead of Jack. Then we set about Operation False Recovery. Waterproof mascara? Check. Kleenex in back pocket? Check. False smile? Check. Ability to hold 30 minute conversation without crying or vomiting? Check (just).

We saw nine people over two days and luckily managed to recruit someone. It was a lovely, down-to-earth girl called Nicola who ticked all of our boxes and then some. She was quietly confident and creativity ran through her veins as strongly as sadness was running through mine. She also came with a real professional integrity and we felt sure she would help Firebelly reach new heights. When Gillie called and offered her the job I felt a delicious sense of distraction. Wouldn't it be great to have Nicola on our team? She was just what we needed. But no sooner had these thoughts touched down in my head, than they were shoved aside by the impending doom of Jack And His Decision.

During the Week From Hell my friends were amazing.

One hundred percent dedicated to distracting me from contacting Jack. One day, Ella, a great friend of mine and Gillie's, phoned to say she was coming over. "Right now. I'm coming over right now!". Gillie and I had originally met Ella at a ludicrously boring arts seminar a few years ago. We'd spotted her with some relief across the room – one of the only other people under fifty – and she had a broad smile, cropped, pixie hair, funky clothes and multi-coloured piercings sprinkled over her entire being. She'd obviously clocked us too because by lunchtime she'd grabbed us at the buffet table and thoughtfully demonstrated her ability to transform paper plates and plastic forks into pretty radical puppets. How could we not like this girl?

Twenty minutes after the phone call she turned up on my doorstep, waving three theatre tickets in our faces. "Come on! We're going to see *Chitty Chitty Bang Bang* and I want to hear no more about it!" She was truly beaming and hopping up and down in her patchwork dungarees until we grabbed our coats and followed her madness. She packaged us into her tiny white van, which was painted with brightly coloured flowers, and we zipped into town whilst Ella chatted manically about flying cars and whistling candy. When we got there, the girls treated me to boxes of popcorn, fluorescent fizzy drinks and a show programme, knowing that a trip to the theatre would have usually had me singing in the aisles and swearing I was born to be a chorus dancer. But this time the best it got out of me was heaving sobs and wet hankies on the final number. But let's be honest here, we all knew it was just a matter of killing that demon called time until I saw Jack again.

So after what felt like about seventy three years, that day came. I was at Gillie's, waiting for Jack to send me a text and let me know when he was back at our house. We were going to meet there and talk. Sleep had escaped me the night before, despite handfuls of herbal sleeping pills, a whole bottle of Chardonnay and being curled up in front of Gillie's flickering open fire. But right now my eyes were wide and my heart stretched so awake it hurt. The text finally came – *'I'm home'* - and I fell into Gillie as if it was the last time I was going to see her. "You'll be alright". She said. "Just call me if you need me and I'll be straight there."

Somehow I found my way into my car and miraculously remembered how to drive.

The only way I lasted the ten minute journey, was to find a quietly supportive voice inside and arrange for it to say: *There is nothing to be scared of. This is Jack, the man you've been with for seven years. Your best friend. Just get there.*

REUNION_

I GOT THERE.

I got home.

I opened the door.

I looked at the dog.

I looked at Jack.

I hugged him.

I hugged him more.

I sat down.

His olive skin was eerily pale and his usually stocky frame seemed slighter. Dark circles had formed around his eyes and his thick black hair was a mess. I think I loved him more than ever in that second before he spoke.

"It's been hard, hasn't it?" Jack said.

"Yes. It's been . . . impossible."

"I just want to say sorry Jess, for this coming out of the blue. It must have been a big shock. I didn't want to hurt you."

His words were comforting but his tone was cold and he wasn't even looking at me. He was looking at the floor. I wanted to hold his hand so much. "I know. I'm glad you told me, really. It hurts like mad, but I'm glad you were honest and told me what you were feeling." Silence. Still looking at the floor. So I shakily asked the question I needed to ask: "What are you feeling now?"

A deep breath. In. Out.

"I'm going to keep being honest. I'm still not sure if I love you." My heart sank to new depths, but I also sensed something hopeful in his voice. "But I think seven years is a lot to give up on. I don't want to just throw it out of the window."

Neither do I, neither do I, neither do I.

"Okay, so what does that mean?"

"I don't know."

And from there he launched into the feelings he'd had during the week. He felt like the life we'd built together had been created by me, not him – that it didn't really belong to him at all; that I had a tendency to lead on everything we did; that without me he'd be nothing and that made him feel empty inside; that he didn't really own any part of his life.

I can't even begin to describe how much this hurt me. I reeled out a film of our life together in my head and found key scenes where he'd made a big decision or when I felt he'd led me. Like when he helped me get work at a local college; like when he'd decided we should get a dog; like when he asked me to marry him. Yep, come to think of it, that was a pretty big thing that he took the lead on.

Hadn't I tried hard over the years to give him all the space he needed? Hadn't I let him chase every opportunity? Hadn't I always been supportive and loving and caring and downright bloody amazing? What was wrong with him? Couldn't he see that I was the greatest fiancée on earth?

We talked for hours until our throats were dry and the night was closing in. Eventually he said he did have a suggestion for what we could do next. Hallelujah. Please say it involves forgetting any of this ever happened.

"Jess, I don't know what I want, but I do know what I don't

want. I don't want to be engaged. I don't want to have a mortgage. I don't want to live out here in the sticks."

"So?"

He rested his head in his hands and continued to talk to the floor. "So, maybe we could sell the house, call off the engagement and move to a rented flat in the city. We could see how things go. There would be work for me at the city theatres. Maybe I could get an agent and really make a go of acting. I can't make any guarantees Jess, but I don't want to throw away seven years just like that."

I stood up, nodded my head and paced around the room. This was good. This was really good. He didn't want to break up. He was willing to stick with the relationship. He even had new ideas for us. Fantastic. So why didn't I feel like jumping up and down in celebration? More to the point – why didn't I feel like I could run over there and smother him in kisses?

Bloody hell, what was I thinking? He was asking me to give up everything to move to a life I didn't want, just in the vague hope that he might love me again. I tried to picture myself in this new life. Jess taking off her engagement ring. Jess moving out of her beloved cottagey home. Jess moving into a city flat. Jess and Jack going out to a city pub with city friends, pretending everything is fine when the whole time Jess is wondering if Jack will love her when he comes back from the bar. Jess's birthdays, Jack's birthdays, Christmases, new years, anniversaries, all haunted by wondering when love is going to walk in again and make everything alright.

It seemed to me that the life I was imagining was exactly like the Week From Hell. Only instead of a week, there was no time limit. It could go on for weeks, months, years, or maybe he'd never get round to loving me again. For the last week I'd been a shadow of who I really was and didn't want to imagine how stretching that time would damage me. How would I possibly stand upright? I'd be some sort of flimsy, cardboard cut-out of who I used to be. How would I ever recover myself if he did – after all – decide he couldn't love me again?

Eventually he tore his eyes away from the floor and lifted his head from his hands.

"I'm sorry Jess. I can't think of anything else. I just can't. All I know for certain is . . ." And at this point he made eye contact for the first time in the whole conversation. "I don't love you."

Well that just did it. If the only thing he could say to me whilst looking me straight in the eye was 'I don't love you' then I had to read the bloody signs, didn't I? I can't remember exactly how or in what order things progressed from there but I think it was something like: hysteria from me, sobbing from him, silence from both of us, the words *we have to break up* somehow escaping my mouth, copious swearing from him, agreement from him, tears, cuddles, snot, apologies, long, sad looks from both of us and – ultimately – parting words.

"I love you in so many ways, Jess, but just not the right way."

"I know. I do know. I think you're stupid. I will always love you but I think you're stupid. You do know you'll never find anyone like me, don't you?"

"Yes. I know."

We were both shaking and could hardly let go of each other. He left the house hunched and shivering with his blue sports bag, a pocketful of tissues and the reddest eyes ever. This was it.

Seven years.

Over. Over. Over.

CHOOSE TO LISTEN_

LINDY WAS CONFUSED.

"You mean, you just let him walk away? Just like that?"

"Yes. I suppose I did." Jess said.

"But, well, I mean, weren't you together for seven years?" Lindy felt a bit rude questioning this perfect stranger but already found herself wrapped up in the story. "Engaged. A business. A home. A dog. Did you really both just give up?"

Jess took a deep breath, paused for second, then let it out, long and slow. She turned to Lindy and spoke across the top of the yellow flames. "It didn't feel like giving up. It felt like something irreversible had happened. And when he asked me to compromise my whole life for a flimsy hope – a hope I knew, at the core of me, I didn't believe in – I just couldn't do it."

Lindy nodded. She could understand that. But having the strength to do it was another matter entirely. Just recently, in Lindy's lowest, darkest moments, she'd felt her strength slip quietly away. And with it, her integrity, her truth. How on earth had Jess managed to call upon all of those resources at her darkest time? It seemed impossible.

Perhaps Jess could hear Lindy's thoughts. "If there's something I learned at that time, it's that at your most horrible, god-awful, soul-wrenching moments, there's always a tiny voice inside of you telling you exactly what you need to do. You might not want to listen to it. And you might let the tears or the drama or the chaos drown it out, but you can choose to let it speak. You can choose to listen."

"Choose to listen . . ." Lindy echoed softly, whispering it to herself. Then a strong blast of cool air rushed in from the waves and jolted her back to life. She turned to Jess. "And that's what you did? When Jack asked you to change everything?"

Jess pulled her hood up over her head, drawing the edges in around her face to keep warm.

"I did. I didn't know that's what I was doing. But I did."

LONDON_

NEXT THING I knew I was in London.

Thank god for credit cards. Thank god for younger brother who lives in London. Thank god for friends who pack your bags, take you to the station and push you onto a train bound for anywhere apart from where you are now.

When I think about those first few days in London, I remember a big blur of sopping wet footsteps on damp, grey streets, and dark, pendulous clouds bumping into the tops of looming tower blocks. I tried to find something to do whilst my brother, Max, worked through the day but I didn't exactly have the boundless motivation required. The January drizzle soaked right into my skin and it felt like my brain was turning as mushy as the newspapers lying in the gutters. I would stand in front of famous attractions and appeal to an unknown force to make me feel something. Anything. But the best I managed was staring at the London Eye until I felt dizzy and slumping over an over-priced cuppa in Covent Garden for six whole hours.

It was about this time I realised it was possible to be overwhelmed with nothingness. It can actually fill you up. I even stopped crying. What was the point? I didn't panic about work or how Gillie would manage Firebelly without me; I didn't miss my friends or my dog or even Jack; and I didn't even want to go shopping, despite having access to all my credit cards and some of the best shopping streets in the world. No, I found it hard to believe I had ever felt anything. Love, lust, indifference. Even my physical senses were dulled. I didn't care when I got soaked in the rain, when my hair stuck to my cheeks and my streaked mascara would have made Alice Cooper proud. And I felt nothing when my brother hugged me on arrival at King's Cross. I had no appetite, no thoughts, no nothing.

"Jess, you can't last like this forever. You look terrible and you're all skin and bones. You're supposed to be here for a relaxing break and you're going to end up going home looking like a half-dead hobo. Here. Get this down you."

I was at Max's flat after a hard day staring into space. A mug of hot steaming tea appeared under my nose. Sugary. It made me want to puke. But I took it and hugged it and stared at my brother. His hair curled over a brow creased with concern. He propped his chin up on his hands, elbows on the table of his tiny kitchenette, and I noticed the strawberry-coloured freckles we shared on our cheeks.

"I think you should hook up with some of your London friends while you're here. They will want to know you're okay. Vicky and Dean don't live far from here."

"Vicky and Dean . . ." I repeated faintly, nodded slowly and sipped some tea. Vicky and Dean were two of my best friends in the whole world. They were possibly my favourite couple ever. Vicky was soft and cuddly, loving and calming and Dean witty and sharp, clever and humble. Trouble was, they were Jack's best friends too.

Over the years we had studied, lived, worked and holidayed together. I suppose you could say we were 'couple' friends. You know what I mean: clinking glasses, hilarious punch lines, and affectionate squeezes all round. It's enough to make any single person retch to within an inch of their lives. But now – and here's where it struck me for the first time – the four of us would not be together anymore.

And that's when I realised just how many friendships were over because of Jack. A whole network of friends built up over the last seven years suddenly ripped away from me. How fucking dare he? What the hell was I supposed to do now? I couldn't possibly look any of these people in the eye. What would they think of me? Of the whole situation?

Anyway the next day my brother packed me off to Vicky and Dean's flat in North London. I didn't put up much of a struggle as I was continuing my efforts towards the title of Most Vacant Person on Earth. When Vicky picked me up from the train station she hugged my pathetic frame. Her hair tickled my face, her skin felt like velvet against my cheek and I felt warmth flood through me. She drew back and looked at me with her gingery eyes. "It's okay sweetheart" she whispered. She smelled so good. Just like old friends.

We got to her flat which was decorated in a deep, spicy orange and smelled of cinnamon incense. She sat me down in the middle of a plump sofa with yet another cup of sweet tea (I swear I could have turned into a bloody cup of tea) and looked at me. She asked soft questions and allowed me all the time I needed to explain what had happened. It was hard to know where to start but everything Vicky said and did made it seem that little bit easier.

Eventually Dean arrived back from work and after welcoming me with a slow hug, he lingered in his soft, lumbering way. Nodding thoughtfully from the dusky corner of the living room, twisting his black curly hair around his thumb and sweeping his eyes across to me gently. There was something unspoken between him and Vicky, like a hushed love for me that spoke volumes in this nurtured quiet. And so I felt utterly protected in the wonderfully soft cocoon it created, which seemed to exist strangely in this tiny North London flat.

These were my friends. Not 'our' friends, not Jack's and Jess's. Mine. They loved Jess for Jess and as I talked I realised that I was scratching the surface of a whole new world here. It scared the hell out of me because I loved all of my friendships exactly how they were. I hadn't asked for them to change. Yet here I was, uttering words I never thought I'd be saying about Jack and I, and with every word something new was emerging.

So I suppose that's when feeling flooded back into me. In London. In Vicky and Dean's tiny flat. The nothingness sneaked out the back door and the emotions slammed though the front. It wasn't fucking easy to be feeling heartbreak and sadness at the same time as love, curiosity and anticipation. But there they were. Taking residence in my head and my heart for the foreseeable future.

And if I couldn't rely on my old friends to see me through that, then who could I rely on?

THE BATH_

WHEN THE TRAIN pulled up in Newcastle station, I saw Gillie waiting for me on the platform.

She was wrapped in a dramatic floor-length cardigan with a scarlet scarf and gloves. Jesus, that girl knew how to do winter. She had Dinah with her and when I stepped off the train, it was my gorgeous little dog who saw me first. She strained on the lead to greet me so I rushed over, collapsed down and ruffled her fur. Then Gillie knealt down and grabbed me for a hug too so that we were entwined in a human / dog / dramatic cardigan combo. "I'm so glad you're ok . . . you're still standing!" Gillie squealed.

"Of course I'm still standing." I got up to show Gillie I was well and truly on two feet. "I'm fine. I've had a good time. Really."

"Okay, but you look dreadful. have you eaten at all while you've been away? Let's get you home so you can scoff some Super Noodles or something."

All the way back in the car, Gillie chatted hurriedly, drummed her fingers on the steering wheel and asked questions about my trip. I answered with as much enthusiasm as I could muster, trying to show her the trip had done me some good despite my rapidly diminishing figure. At least the nodding, staring and occasional drooling had come to an end. And actually I did feel all right. I felt quite calm and quite good and quite strong actually. Maybe the change of scenery had been medicinal after all.

As we pulled up outside my home, Gillie stopped the engine, turned to me and took a deep breath. *Here we go*, I thought, *here's the breaking news*. "Look, Jess, you need to know what Jack's been doing for the last few days. He's been into the house and taken some of his things, so don't get a shock when you see all the gaps and spaces. And he's moved in with a mate in the city. He'll be there for a while."

I nodded and stared at the dashboard. "Good. He's got somewhere to go. That's good." I tried to blot out the fact that I now had to hear about Jack's whereabouts through a third party. Gillie grabbed my hand and squeezed it and I swallowed back the tears. "Good. Excellent. Thanks for telling me Gillie."

From that moment on I had only one thing on my mind and it wasn't bloody Super noodles. I needed a hot bath. So I dumped my stuff in the kitchen, found some candles, put on some music and got that water running. I ignored any recently formed gaps on shelves, in cupboards, in drawers, in my belly, and just concentrated on getting into that bath.

When I dipped into the water it was so deliciously warm I could have melted. The scent of lavender soothed me, and I listened to the bubbles crackle gently around my ears. The muscles in my neck started to soften and as I closed my eyes I could sense the orangey-black flicker of the candles against the glossy surface of the bathroom tiles. Distantly, I could hear the words of family and friends playing quietly as a background to my thoughts. Overlapping and wrapping around me like a blanket. Silken. Tranquil. Tender.

The music I'd put on drifted through to the bathroom and

spoke words of loss. I felt the haunting tones of the man's voice filter into me and I was there with him.

'And I am trying to glow in the darkness of your old love . . . but it seeps slowly through the cracks we made and I'm lost . . . I'm lost . . . "

The tears were flowing into the bath before I knew what was happening. But this time they weren't painful or sharp. They were soft and true. They were silent and real. They flowed into the bath like a tap and everything felt so watery and silky and warm. My lips, my nose, my eyes, my ears, my knees, my elbows, my toes, all seemed to be part of this magnificent outpour. I hadn't known it before but these tears were the real ones.

Now I was really crying.

Now I was really listening.

Somehow that night I hauled myself out of the heaviness of my watery haven and into bed.

Then I slept. I slept long and peaceful and deep and my head forgot that my heart was breaking. And in the morning I awoke to the light of day streaming through my very empty house.

It was a long time before I ventured into the world of hot baths again. Although there had been something terrifyingly purging about that night, it was not something I wanted to revisit right away.

Instead my days gave in to the robotics of shuffling around the house, shuffling around at work and shuffling out for walks with the dog. Everything was safe and everything was empty. Everything was quiet and everything was hollow. My friends kept a close eye on me yet gave me a wide berth when they decided that was what I needed. I was grateful.

I was in no fit state to decide what I needed.

THE WALK_

EVENTUALLY IT WAS NOT a question of what I needed, but what my bank balance needed.

There was still an engaged couple's bills to pay. Not to mention the debt that was stacking up. So the inevitability of meeting Jack smacked me in the face. It was time.

God, if there's ever a thing that goes into a girl's top ten of most undesirable things to do, it is Talking Through Finances With Your Ex. Nevertheless, Jack turned up as arranged one misty day in February, and stood on his own doorstep, knocking on the door like a stranger.

I stumbled through the surreal niceties of inviting him in and making him a cup of tea. Dinah pawed up at him as if she hadn't seen him in a thousand years and he knelt down to tickle her pot-belly. I watched as I automatically stirred his three sugars into his double-strength tea and wondered if I lay like that would he tickle my belly too?

We sat in the living room. Him on the sofa in the exact spot where he'd told me he didn't love me anymore. Me on a cushion on the floor, preferring to keep my distance from re-enacting the fateful day. First of all we talked about work. He asked me how

Firebelly was getting on (not a bloody clue), if we'd managed to recruit a new artist (some girl called Nicola?) and if I was working on any interesting projects (erm, me? Work?). He even commented that I looked great having lost a bit of weight which felt momentarily euphoric before I remembered love isn't forged by protruding ribs.

He eventually tore his eyes away from my ribs, took a deep breath and announced that, in view of his change of heart about life and pretty much everything, he'd decided to leave the company.

I'd been expecting this announcement and wondered where exactly his heart was these days if it wasn't with me and it wasn't with the job.

Then we went on to matters pending. Mortgage: he was willing to hand the house over to me without me buying him out, as long as I took on our hefty bunch of joint loans. That would just about even out the debt. He said he'd been watching a programme on the telly about this kind of thing and that we'd need to get a solicitor to help us have a separation agreement drawn up. Bloody hell, a separation agreement.

Talk about closure.

After the absurdity of all the financial stuff, I suggested we go for a walk. I didn't want to cross into any matters of the heart whilst we were sitting here like this, sipping tea with the fog crawling up against the window. We would be trapped in our own words, unable to start, end or make sense of anything. No, a walk was a better idea. A walk has a beginning and an end. A walk gives you the comfort of that. So while Jack packed up more stuff from what used to be our home, I sat out in the car and waited for him. I gripped the steering wheel and stared at the mucky dashboard. Dinah panted in the back, excited at the prospect of an excursion with mummy and daddy.

If only she knew.

We drove to a nearby meadow and Dinah leapt out of the

car. She bounded off as if it was a summer's day, whilst we walked behind her, through the falling fog and the dewy, knee-high grass. I was painfully aware of the proximity of Jack and fought against the seven-year instinct to grab his hand.

Jack wanted to know how I'd been and what I'd been up to. I was tempted to say, *well, actually Jack, I've hardly slept a wink in weeks, a hot bath makes me cry an ocean, and eating a good meal is a thing of the past.* But instead I mumbled something about London and that seemed to be enough.

Jack had been looking for a new job. Jack had found a new job in the pub we'd been at on New Year's Eve. It offered bed and board and a basic salary so all in all Jack seemed to be doing fine. But Jack was thin and pale and jolty and I knew he was 'doing fine' in the sense that I, too, was 'doing fine'.

As we walked, I realised that this might be the last time that I would actually get to talk to him with any degree of truth. I panicked. I took advantage of it.

"Jack, I understand that we can't be together anymore and I want to believe that everything will be all right. But I can't picture it. I can't picture me without you."

"I know Jess. I'm so sorry. You did mean the world to me once." Jack drew me in to him and let me cry against him. As we stood hugging on the murky hillside, I could feel his chest rising and falling as I sobbed deeper into it. The fog circled and prodded us with its bleak, curling fingers. I asked him a hundred different questions through my tears, barely even aware I was saying them out loud.

"Why did you leave me? What's wrong with me? Will you ever come back?" He squirmed and fidgeted under my grip but I kept crying like a ferocious child. And I didn't ever want to move. I didn't ever want to run out of questions because that would mean he'd let go of me and I'd be alone again.

"Why did you ever ask me to marry you if you didn't mean it?"

And then he did let go of me, grabbed my shoulders and looked me straight in the eyes. "Now hang on a minute. I did bloody well mean it at the time and you know it. How can you ask me that?" He whipped away from me and stormed into the fog.

I stuttered and aimed at his back, "But when you ask that question it's supposed to be a guarantee. You're supposed to love me forever."

He spun round and came at me with blazing black eyes. His neck was tense, his jaw tight and his step was quick through the grass. He grabbed me by the shoulders again but shook me hard this time, his fingers gripping painfully. He breathed in and I knew he was about to say something to pierce me right through. This was our pattern. This was what we did. But, just as quickly as it had arrived, his fury died away. And he dropped his hands.

"Jess, you have to get over this and figure out what it is you want. What do you want?" There was a suspended silence and then he started walking again when he realised the only answer he was going to get was one he didn't want to hear.

I stood for a few moments in a daze, watching him grow more and more distant. Eventually, after he disappeared over a hill, I followed him. On and on through that awful foggy place, trawling through long, wet grasses and ducking under low, sagging trees until I finally ended up where we'd started. The dog was circling the car like a homing pigeon, and Jack leant against the passenger door, sucking on a cigarette. "Oh my god, Jack. The dog. What shall we do about Dinah?"

Jack looked at her and sighed. "I think it's best she stays with you."

I felt a rush of gratitude because I needed Dinah with me. But there was also a simultaneous rush of sorrow. How could it be so easy for him to let her go? But then, it made sense because he was letting everything else go too.

And that was that.

Walk over. Conversation over.

I drove Jack to a nearby bus stop, got out of the car and hugged him one last time before he went. I watched him walk down the road, two big bags in tow and a rucksack on his back. He looked like a character from a fairytale about to embark on some adventure in a far-off land.

And I suppose, in a way, he was.

A SPARKLE_

THERE COMES A VERY strange time when you've just split up with the love of your life.

The point when everybody expects you to be better. For a long time they have been hoping that your hurt will stop, that the rapid weight loss will stop and that the incessant crying will stop. But there comes a time when those hopes turn to expectations.

That is the time I am talking about.

I noticed that encouraging smiles were starting to fade and that my friends looked almost as knackered as me. I started thinking about the girl I was before Jack and I had split up. Apart from being the most fantastic fiancée known to man, I had also been fun, energetic and motivated. I had been a businesswoman, a leader, an artist. Where had that person gone?

Did I want her back?

Well, if it was a choice between that and continuing to be the sorry soul that I was at the moment, then the answer was yes, I bloody did want her back. So the initiation began. A couple of nights out on the town. Some small but square meals. Answering the phone at work. Attending meetings. Organising projects. At first it felt like I was scraping the bottom of the barrel for my smiles, my words, my conviction. But as I fell into the land of the living I suppose I started to rediscover some of the tiny beauties about, well, living.

It wasn't that I didn't miss Jack. I missed him terribly and the nights were the worst. But the days were starting to feel better. When I faced challenges at work Gillie stopped hovering around me ready to pick me up if I fell apart, and I started to face them on my own. Slowly I became recognisable as Jess again. The Jess with clout. The Jess with passion.

And then came the challenge of all challenges. Ella had yet another crazy idea that we should all go to a rock concert together – how the hell did she keep picking up these tickets to random events? I agreed despite the fact I didn't like rock music. In fact I hated it. But I thought what the hell - this could be the ultimate test for me. Mosh around in a sweaty pit with a gang of hairy rockers? Bring. It. On.

So I pulled on my skinny jeans (bearing in mind skinny was a look I did scarily well these days) and a slash-backed t-shirt with a metal dog collar. I ruffled my hair, smudged my eye make-up and set off with Gillie and Ella in the taxi. I have to admit that on the way there I felt like I was riding to my death or something. All those people. All that noise. Could my battered nervous system really take it? But when we got out of the taxi, Gillie and Ella each linked arms with me and marched me into the dingy concert hall like I was the rock star.

And we had an amazing time. We glugged lager as if it were going out of fashion and moshed with the best of the hard-core rockers. I remember feeling an unexpected sense of release that night. A release of inhibition. A release of worry. A release of expectation. Okay, so maybe it only lasted as long as a few rock songs, but it was definitely there and definitely had something to do with the release of Jack.

At the end of the night the three of us tumbled out of the

taxi and into my house. Dinah greeted us enthusiastically and we took her for a drunken walk. As we giggled our way round the fields near my housing estate, I thought, this is it. This is what it's all about. Walking with your mates in the moonlight after a night out. It was so totally messy, yet so totally precious.

The three of us managed to squeeze into my bed and whispered like kids until we finally fell asleep. In the morning we woke up in a haze of cups of tea and knotted hair, ruffled bed sheets and twisted pyjamas. We recalled moments from the night before in fits of laughter and confusion. And it wasn't until we'd been lying there for half an hour that I realised what day it was today.

Valentine's Day. Oh god.

Before I could even begin to feel sorry for myself, Ella shoved something into my hand. "This arrived for you." She flashed a cheeky smile and sat back to watch me. It was a home-made card with a photo of me and Dinah glued to the front, decorated with sequin hearts and pink glitter. I looked at Ella and hugged her with my eyes. "Happy Valentine's Day." She said.

So what if it was Valentine's Day? I was going to have a brilliant day by myself. So I rescued an old dress from the back of the wardrobe – one that Jack had always cringed at because it was so tight - and pulled it on. It was a little denim number with short rouched sleeves, a leather tie at the waist and it was much looser now but Jack wasn't going to bloody well see that. I wore it over loose black trousers and shuffled on some sparkly pumps. Nice. Even if I did say so myself.

And out I went to face the world as a single person on Valentine's Day.

On my way to work I stopped at a local café and bumped into Marcus, Gillie's boyfriend of six years.

We stood at the counter together as I ordered a skinny latté and we chatted about work and a few projects we had on the go. He ran a drama and arts company called 'Play The Fool' which was fitting because he had always reminded me somehow of an old-fashioned circus clown. He had plenty of charisma wrapped up in a small, skinny frame, brown spiky hair and a slightly wonky smile which was always preceded by his green eyes snapping to life. A very jolly soul but by god he could be fickle and erratic. Sometimes it was unsettling to be around him.

And for that reason, among others, I have to admit I had problems with Marcus. They stretched years back and were mainly based on the way he treated Gillie. Yes he was charming and quirky, and Gillie always insisted she was blissfully happy, but I sensed an undertone that something wasn't quite right. And I'd never felt it was my place to have it out with him so we were civil to each other because of Gillie. Today though, we were having a nice chat and nothing was going to spoil my good mood.

My latté turned up and I made to leave but Marcus gently placed his hand on my arm to stop me. "Jess, I just have to say you look absolutely beautiful today. Is there something up?"

See? How unsettling is that? "No, there's nothing up." I said, trying to hide my embarrassment.

"There is definitely something different. A sparkle in your eye. Anyway, see you later!" He gave me a little wink and trotted off to find a table with his coffee in one hand, newspaper tucked under his arm and whistling some chirpy little tune. I stared after him for a few seconds but then snapped myself out of it and left the café.

As I stepped outside I thought about what he'd said and a smile spread across my lips. Whatever I thought of Marcus, I knew he didn't give compliments freely. And I thought maybe there is something up actually. Maybe there is a sparkle in my eye. It was then I could feel something rising from the pit of my stomach, and for the first time in weeks it wasn't depression or sickness or longing. It was something very different. It was warm and it was welcome. It didn't feel very familiar. In fact it felt brand new. A new kind of happiness that started on the inside and worked its way out. I shivered and sipped my latté.

Weird. Jess feeling little bits of happiness.

What on earth would happen next?

PERSONAL DEVELOPMENT SWOTS_

WHEN THE PHONE rang in the office that morning it was good news.

Gillie and I had been awarded places on a business development course which we'd applied for ages ago and almost forgotten about. It seemed like a good idea at the time and it seemed like an even better idea now, especially considering one of Firebelly's Managing Directors had just walked off in a strop.

When our information packs arrived through the post we leafed through them. Social enterprise – good. Fundraising – useful. Business planning – excellent. Finance and accounting – stupidly boring but necessary. But oh god, what was that on the first day? Personal development. Shit.

A whole day of personal development. How the hell was I going to get through that? Revealing my secrets to perfect strangers? Yelling at myself in a mirror? Shouting self-indulgent affirmations led by some power-suited, overly-coiffed, equally self-indulgent guru? No. Thank. You.

We frantically tore through the pages of the info pack and searched for another option, a way to escape, but it appeared there was no way we could sneak out of it. The course had been paid for through funders and if we didn't turn up on the first day they wouldn't let us do the rest of it. So Gillie and I agreed to turn up, keep our heads down and mouths shut. Hopefully nobody would notice us and we could just make use of the free coffee and cakes.

So when we arrived the following week, we found an inconspicuous place to sit in the small, grey conference room and drank our coffees silently. So far, so good. No eye contact made with anyone. No mirrors. No self indulgent affirmations.

After ten minutes or so the room was full and people were chatting in low, guarded tones. Judging by the body language and regular glances at the door it was pretty obvious everybody felt the same way as us. So it made me wonder what the point was in all this personal development malarkey, if nobody actually wanted to do it.

Just as I was thinking that, a man on the other side of the room stood up and made his way to the front. I wondered what the hell he was doing as it was obvious we would be starting as soon as the facilitator arrived. He took a deep breath and everybody looked up at him.

"Hi, I'm Ben." Oh god, I thought, do we all have to get up and do that? He looked around at us all. I felt for him, I really did, but there was no way I was getting up to do the same thing. I just didn't have it in me today.

"Before we start, I just want to say that today is going to be really easy and gentle. On this course, we believe that a successful business can't exist without successful people. And successful people are usually happy people."

Oh. I see. He *is* the facilitator. Oops.

As he continued, I watched Ben carefully. I searched for any signs of self-importance. Perhaps even a flicker? But I just couldn't find them. In fact, as the morning wore on, I found exactly the opposite. And he was nothing like what I expected of a personal development guru. He didn't wear a shiny suit or have a tendency to do air punches. No. Ben was the most normal man you'd ever see. Soft white hair, light blue eyes, a friendly smile and plenty of interesting things to say.

By lunchtime I was totally won over.

But perhaps I was alone in this because around the room were still lots of hunched shoulders, still lots of low voices and still no eye contact. I looked over at Gillie who was sitting on the edge of a desk, munching on a sandwich and chatting to some tall, gangly bloke with spiky hair. She looked like I felt. Relaxed and comfortable, with a sense of curiosity.

In the afternoon, there was still no yelling at mirrors or revealing of dark secrets. Everything we did was personal and reflective and felt very, very safe. Ben was gently pushing me into honest judgement of Firebelly and also of myself. I found myself scribbling away furiously, trying to capture what was going on in the room. This was good stuff.

At the end of the day, we each got given a piece of paper, which read across the top: *I commit to 100 days of positive action.* "That's the real challenge," Ben said, "to practice with working positivity into your everyday thoughts and actions." Well I was on a roll now so I gleefully picked up my pen to sign on the dotted line. Just as I was about to scribble my name in a celebrity-like fashion, I noticed the whole group halt. Everyone except me, Gillie and gangly, spiky-haired bloke looked totally appalled.

A tiny wiry woman shrieked from the back of the room "Do we have to sign this?"

Ben smiled. "No. You don't have to." The woman huffed and puffed and screwed up her twitchy little nose, shoving the bit of paper back into her file without signing it. The rest of the group followed her example. But Gillie and I totally signed the paper.

And that, we reckoned, made us official personal development swots.

THE DIAMOND IN THE TEAR_

THAT EVENING I went back to work to do my usual Thursday night drama workshop with twenty eight hyper-energetic children.

The session was fab. It was the first time I'd managed to lead things on my own since Jack had gone, and I actually felt quite on top of things. All the kids went home laughing and happy.

One hundred days of positive action here I come.

As I was driving home I rolled down the car window and breathed in the cold, fresh air. I flicked on the radio and a soft chill-out tune filled the car as I relaxed into my seat. For the first time in my Jackless life I was actually looking forward to going back to my lovely little home. And there was something about this night that was alerting my senses. The music seemed rich and alive, the breeze brushed my face like a thousand tiny feathers and as I drove I was noticing all kinds of things. Spinning patterns in the clouds. Swooping flocks of birds in the sky. A bright light on the horizon. In fact, the light on the horizon really caught my attention because it was bright neon pink. What on earth was it? I leaned forward and tried to identify it. It was . .

. oh fuck it . . . it was the sign for the Cantonese restaurant . . . where Jack had proposed to me four years ago.

It all came flooding back and I was in that moment again. The way he'd been chewing on a prawn cracker. The way he'd looked at me with love and complete tenderness. And those gorgeous, perfect words . . .

"Will you marry me?"

The way the deep red and velvety purple décor of the restaurant had sloshed around in teary waves as I held my breath in adoring stupor. The words tumbling from my lips, "Yes, yes of course I'll marry you." Our hands clasping at each other, our foreheads locked together in the blissful secrecy of the moment we were in and the delicate scent of the Cantonese food marking the memory.

We were so lost in the world we'd just created . . . in the world we'd just changed with a few tiny words. God, it had been beautiful.

But now, driving the car, my chest heaved, my shoulders shook and my eyes streamed in mourning of that moment. It had seemed so real and full and true but now it meant nothing. I cried into the night and the pink sign on the horizon disappeared into a pool of neon sadness. I would never be that happy again. I would never know what it was like to be so loved, so adored. How could everything still be occurring? Why was the restaurant still there? How was the world still turning?

When I heard myself wailing like a child from the very depths of my empty belly, I was scared. That cry didn't sound like anyone who was ever going to feel goodness again. I felt like I was floating above the car, drifting along the road, and willing my fractured self to get home safely. It was like the only way to deal with this hurt was to look at it from above and see that what I needed to do was get the car home and call someone.

I watched myself pull into the driveway, unlock the door and collapse onto the kitchen floor. I saw myself sitting there, heaving and wretching in the darkness and all the time I could hear this terrible wailing. How could I stop it? I willed myself to pick up my mobile phone and flick through some contacts.

Gillie: no answer. Ella: no answer. I couldn't leave a message in this state. Mam and dad: no, it would scare them to death. Marcus: bloody hell, I must be desperate. And all the time I'm whispering to myself, *not Jack, not Jack. I know you want to, but not Jack.*

Max: No answer. Vicky: no answer. Wails louder now. An agony was binding my torso and squeezing a horrific sound from inside. I needed to get through to someone. Anyone. But I'd exhausted all possibilities and Jack was starting to look like the only option. Before I could live with the regret I speed-dialled his number and waited to be connected, not even knowing what I was going to say or what good this would do. But if I could just hear his voice maybe everything would be okay. I heard the distant clicking of phone lines doing their thing, the almost-silent buzz of a connection about to be made . . . *please god get me through this . . . please god . . .*

And then something very odd happened. My consciousness swooped back into my body and I felt a particularly large, hot tear burn gradually down my cheek and swing on the end of my chin in slow motion. I hung up the phone and crouched absolutely still. I felt the tear bob and sway until it parted contact with my skin and I saw it drop slowly, reluctantly towards the floor, its shape billowing until it finally hit the surface, the heat and sadness of the tear colliding with the coldness of the laminated floor.

And now the whole world seemed to stop.

No sound. No breath. No movement. Just a tiny puddle shining up at me. And through the darkness of the room, through the halted shadows and the hovering night I could see the pearlescent glow, the unmistakable shine of a diamond. A diamond in the pool of my tear.

I looked at this tiny phenomenon until its shine prickled my eyes and spoke to my heart. It said *you're home, don't worry because you're home.* I didn't question the words I just let them sink into me as if they were filling a deep, cavernous hole. *You're home.* And after what felt like a very long time I started to become vaguely aware of the reality forming around me. My wrists aching, my knees hurting, cars passing by my house, Dinah trotting around in the next room, wondering why I hadn't said hello to her yet. I was home. I was in one piece, I'd stopped crying, and I was home.

I felt very calm and I knew what I needed to do. I needed to walk Dinah, brush my teeth and go to bed. I could do that. Walk, teeth, bed. Some strange force had helped me out here and I wasn't sure what to make of it.

But as long as I could recall the brilliant shine of a diamond caught in the pool of my own tear, I knew I could do what I needed to do.

FORCES_

JESS STOOD UP AFTER THAT, and stretched her hands up to the sky, tiny fountains of sand streamed down around her as she moved.

She stretched carefully to one side, and then the other, before swooping her hands down and massaging the small of her back.

"Ouch," she said. "I must remember to move instead of gabbing on all the time. Starting the new year with a dodgy back isn't in the grand plan."

She trudged back towards the fire and Lindy, and knelt down, her back to the sea. "Am I boring you yet?"

"Nope." Lindy said, honestly. "This fire needs a bit of TLC though."

"True." Jess agreed. So she threw on some of the wood she'd collected earlier and Lindy gave the fire a poke with the stick that was still sitting at her side. "Is it all getting a bit weird? Hearing about my random, spiritual stuff? It's not my usual conversation opener, you know."

Lindy laughed. "I gathered as much. No, it's fine. It's interesting. I'm going through my own stuff right now so . .

." She didn't know what else to say. She'd settled into the comfort of listening and didn't particularly want to change that, but letting Jess know this stuff was helpful seemed important. "Well let's just say it's good to hear that someone else has been through it too. I mean, I know people go through crap every single day but your story is . . . I don't know, it seems like good timing."

Jess laughed deeply. "Oh, good lord, isn't it always about timing?" She asked nobody in particular. "Like on that night when I saw that neon sign of the restaurant where Jack proposed. I drove past the bloody thing every day but on that night, when I was feeling good and had a good energy running through me, that's when I noticed it. That's when my world came crashing down. Yet again."

"It does seem weird," Lindy agreed. "So what was that all about? I would have said the timing was fucking awful."

Even though it was clearly a painful memory for Jess, she still had the shadow of a smile on her lips. "When I look back on it, and the weird thing with the tear on my kitchen floor – I mean, it literally spoke to me Lindy, in the clearest, most direct voice – I think there are so many things about the world that we don't understand. There are forces at work that can help us in ways we can't even imagine . . . it's all about being open to it."

Lindy nodded. She hadn't felt open for months. In fact, she'd felt so clamped shut that she thought any goodness left inside her might never see the light of day again. It wasn't until that evening, fighting back tears and stomping along the beach that the vision of the fire glowing in the alcove had done something to her. And now she was open. Had that been something to do with the forces Jess was talking about?

Jess continued, "When Jack left, I was like a dog with a bone. I wouldn't let go of the pain. I let it engulf me physically, emotionally. In a weird way the pain felt comforting and it was the only thing I could control and call mine. And every time there was a little opening, a little glimmer of light through the sharpness of that pain, it would whack me again, testing my boundaries, pushing me hard. And when I was collapsed on my kitchen floor, making that call to Jack, something had to be done."

Jess threw her hands up to the sky and tipped her head back, "And you did it, didn't you? You bloody well did it."

"Who?" Lindy asked, finding herself again slightly unnerved by Jess's behaviour, "Who did what?"

Jess brought her hands back to her lap. "The universe. Me. God. All of us rolled into one. That tear, that voice, that's what brought me back to reality. Back to myself."

Lindy let out a breath that came right from her belly. "It all seems a bit heavy, don't you think?"

"It could sound that way," Jess said, "But I tell you what, when it happens . . ." Lindy leaned forward, wide eyed, hoping Jess would go on. "It feels light as a feather."

BIRTHDAY WEEKEND_

NOT LONG AFTER the dodgy tear incident, my birthday rolled around.

I wanted to get away from home and work and all things Jack-related so Gillie suggested having a night out with the girls. This immediately conjured visions of luminous alcopops, laddered tights, knotted hair and curiously sticky nightclub floors. No thank you. I wanted calm and relaxation. I wanted a whole weekend away with my girls – Gillie, Ella and Vicky if she could make it up from London.

Bearing in mind my digestive system was barely coping with actual food, it seemed to be the only thing I could stomach anyway. I wanted to drink all the boozy cocktails and eat all the gravy and chips possibly consumable, really I did, but there were some demons at play here that just wouldn't allow it. Where they came from I wasn't sure. Of course, there was part of me that was hoping Jack might hear that I was thin now and come running back into my skinny arms for a massive snog. But there was more to it than that. Hunger had become my friend. That rumbling in my tummy that had once been unpleasant was now a comforting stroke, a tender squeeze to remind me I was sad.

And sadness was something I knew and felt okay with. I wanted the sadness to stay close by and hunger kept it there - lingering and ready to scoop me up when I didn't know what else to do.

And that's why I needed more time around people. People who would look out for me and help me navigate my birthday with a firm love in a gentle way. People who wouldn't stuff cake down my throat to make me gain pounds but instead understand that my recovery was more complex than that.

So I worked all the hours god sent to make sure Gillie and I got our work done in time, spread the word to a few carefully chosen friends and found a beautiful little cottage on the west coast. We arrived on the Friday night in a staggered convoy of cars and a flurry of duvets. We managed to pack twelve of us into three little rooms and promptly turned them into a tightly packed arrangement of air mattresses, pillows and foot pumps.

The first night was perfect.

We sat stuffed shoulder-to-shoulder in the tiny living room, wearing our pyjamas and slippers and putting the world to rights. Everybody else was chewing on great slabs of luke-warm pizza and I tried, I really did, but despite being surrounded by the most glorious and encouraging smiles, I only managed a bit of cucumber and hummus.

We spent most of the night cackling at a deck of porno playing cards, simultaneously sighing at and harshly criticising slushy movies and sniggering into our wine at each other's worst sex stories. Gillie and Ella danced on the furniture to awful music whilst Vicky took on the role of a crazy old dance teacher, demanding they twirl faster and faster. We all laughed until our cheeks ached and our eyes were closing.

The next day was my birthday and I awoke to a cup of tea, a pile of cards and all of the girls sat round me as if I was an installation at a Tracy Emin exhibition. We munched on some toast, yawned, stretched and agreed that the next thing on the agenda was a walk on the beach.

When we got to the beach, the wind was biting, but the sun sliced over the sea in pretty opal shards and I couldn't help but smile behind my scarf. There was only us on the beach. Us and the sun and the wind. We tramped along in our wellies and spaced out in little pairs and groups according to who loved doing what. Some of us paddled. Some of us collected shells or took photos or drew pictures in the sand. Some of us moved forwards in wide strides and some of us plodded slowly along.

I hung back with Ella and we got chatting.

There was something about Ella – ever since the day I had met her at the seminar with the paper plate puppets – that encouraged me to speak truthfully. I knew most people found her a bit wacky, not to mention a permanent source of entertainment, but I'd always seen a soulful side to Ella too. Whenever we got together, we nearly always found ourselves talking about love and life and everything. The only problem with that was that these days, it meant the conversation always came back to my love, my life, my everything: Jack. Or obvious lack of.

I moaned yet again about how hard things were without him and even admitted that his absence was creating the hollowness in my belly, the slightness of my arms. I knew Ella got this. How? Because she's a woman and knows that we are trained from birth to believe that if we stay slim we can have anything. But there she was in front of me, curvy and glorious in her pink, shiny ski-suit of all things, telling me how proud she was of me. "Jess, you've come so far you banana. All this stuff with Jack, you've been ground down to the ground. But now you're rising slowly and you'll build your armour back up when you're ready. Once you remember what an awesome beast you are, the body thing won't matter. At least, not as much.

I knew Ella was right, she'd always been so bloody wise underneath her wild exterior. But there was another reason for my lack of appetite. Something that really made me sick to the stomach. I'd tried to hide it, but if I was honest, I was terrified of Jack finding someone new. I mean, really, horror-movie-heroine terrified. And what's more, there was an extra-special fear that maybe it would . . . dramatic drum roll please . . . turn out to be someone I knew.

"And the thing is Ella – and this makes me feel like a right bitch – is that I keep looking at my friends as if they're all suspects. I keep trying to work out which of them he used to get on with the best, or which of them have something in common with him or which one - and I KNOW it's bloody stupid - which one is the thinnest and sexiest. I fucking hate myself for doing it. But it's an automatic thing. I can't stop."

Ella swung my hand as we walked which made me feel marginally less ugly. "First of all, I'm obviously the thinnest and sexiest and the man now repulses me so he can bloody well jog on."

She gave a little swish of her neon pink, water-repellent hips and smouldered at me until I couldn't help but laugh. "For god's sake, it's perfectly natural. You're just preparing for what you think is the worst thing that can happen. So not a bitch." I gulped back an Olympic-size pool of tears. "But sweet-pea, you have to realise that you can't control what Jack does now. You have to try and find things to fill your time that belong to you. And one day what you are doing will become more important than what he is doing."

Ella was right. Of course she was. But I was in the thick of it now. And as we walked along the beach, and the girls passed me smiling and shouting happy birthday I decided I was a bitch after all. A bitch for suspecting these people could hurt me. A bitch for throwing their kindness back in their face. And maybe it was easier to be that. If I felt ugly and horrible and bitchy then I could understand why Jack wouldn't want to be with me. I could understand why I had no birthday card or phone call from him. I could understand why he would choose one of my thinner, sexier friends instead. And maybe he already had.

God, maybe he already had.

Next we went for drinks in a backwards country pub – the kind where the music screeches to a halt when you walk in and your order of a vodka and lime is met with staggered gasps of horror. But the twelve of us traipsed right in anyway and introduced the locals to our sand-filled hiking socks and pink, wind-snapped cheeks. We did a very noisy and joyful home-made sweepstake on the grand national and I won on a horse called 'Addicted to Love'. Of course I bloody did.

We left in the wake of sighs of relief from the pot-bellied locals. At least we gave them something to talk about. And when I got back to the cottage there were balloons and streamers everywhere, presents in a pile on the floor, glasses of champagne lined up for everyone, three different birthday cakes and a homemade birthday banner penned by Ella. I cried and laughed and slumped into an armchair, spilling the bubbly that was shoved in my hand.

The rest of the weekend passed by in a strange routine of surface sweet moments and dark, ravenous thoughts. All the time I was smiling and acting like the perfect birthday girl. But none of it was enough to stop me from indulging in the thought of Jack shacking up with one of my mates. The thought of it lingered like a shadow, sniggering at me every time it caught me enjoying myself or being tempted by cake. Ella kept giving me reassuring hugs but I didn't have the heart to tell her that every time she did it, the thought just magnified a hundred times and increased my certainty that it would eventually happen.

By the end of the weekend, with a distinct lack of birthday messages from Jack and a heavy heart, I drove back home with a steamed-up car full of friends singing every god-awful girl-power song in the history of pop. And I'd resigned myself to the fact that Jack was going to find someone else. It was going to happen soon. And it was going to be someone I knew. And because I knew it was going to happen, I also knew I was going to be alright.

Because I would be prepared.

So there.

RE-CLAIMING_

WHAT WITH ALL THE ugly thoughts and suspicions, I realised I had fallen slightly behind in the whole '100 days of positive action' thing.

Right. Time to get back on it.

One night, when I'd been moping around the house staring like a tragic film star into the spaces where Jack's stuff used to be, I decided it was time to re-claim the house. First of all I made a point of finding a good solicitor to organise that god-awful separation agreement and to help me re-mortgage the house. It was the only way I was going to be able to afford to live alone. Okay, so the house didn't quite belong to me yet. And there were several thousand – very expensive – hoops I had to jump through before it would. But I could re-claim it in other ways. I could redecorate. I'd always loved painting.

So the living room was the first victim. It wasn't until I started thinking about new colour schemes that I realised that the old colours were all ones Jack had chosen. And if I was really honest, what the fuck had he been thinking? Who puts chocolate brown with slate grey? Ugh. Time for a change.

So I picked out a fresh green for the fireplace wall and a cool apple-white for the other walls. I spent hours doing the boring stuff first: covering the furniture, washing down the walls and introducing all the cracks in the walls to their new best friend, Polyfilla. Then came the sanding of skirting boards, the removal of shelves, the hoovering up of cobwebs and then what felt like a million undercoats to get rid of that bloody horrible brown and grey. But eventually the real painting started and I got lost in the lovely swish swish of soft brush strokes.

Sometimes I'd have some music playing, and because the weather was getting finer, sometimes I'd open the door and let Dinah run in and out of the garden while I worked. It was lovely. This was Jess doing something about her life. This was Jess taking ownership.

After two weeks of an exhausting work / paint schedule, a few stubbed toes on misplaced furniture and three coats of paint on every wall, however, I realised that what I was taking ownership of was a mighty big living room. The swishing of brush strokes suddenly didn't seem so therapeutic, as I realised that this actually was the first room I had ever decorated without Jack. Well there's only one place realisations like that go. And it was a place I knew all about.

But this time, I remembered the night I'd seen that tiny diamond glow in my tears and before my body could relive any further slumping on the floor, I took a strange sort of action.

It just felt like the only thing to do. I stomped through to the spare room and searched through my desk drawers. I knew it was in there somewhere. Where was it? Aha, there it was. A notebook my mam had given me ages ago. A lovely black, fabric covered notebook with bells and buttons and stitching all over the cover.

Untouched and unloved. Until now.

I grabbed a pen and crashed down on the dust-sheet adorned sofa. I wrote furiously across the top of the page:

REASONS WHY BEING YOUNG, FREE & INDEPENDENT IS BLOODY BRILLIANT!:

I didn't have to think about what to write. It just flowed. Okay, so I was shaking as I wrote but it didn't matter because this felt useful.

① I can spend LOADS of time with friends. I can plan to see them or be as spontaneous as I like with surprise visits.

② I only have MYSELF to make plans for, which opens up a million possibilities...

ROCK CONCERTS · PLAYS · MOONLIT WALKS · DRIVES IN THE COUNTRYSIDE · SUNNY PICNICS · NIGHT CLUBS · CINEMA OUTINGS · HOLIDAYS · WEEKENDS AWAY *and more...*

③ I can try out all the things I've always been interested in .... singing, oil painting, dancing, sky diving!

④ I can look at ANY man and not worry about a jealous boyfriend. I can make brilliant new friends without worrying about anybody else's thoughts on the matter.

⑤ I can go to bed as early or as late as I want - messing about and pottering as much as I like.

⑥ I can spend MY money on ANYTHING that takes my fancy. I'm only answerable to myself for my financial decisions.

⑦ I am safe in the knowledge that I CAN cope with what life throws at me. I am resourceful and strong and I can enjoy many aspects of life alone. I am safe and happy in my own skin.

⑧ When I get home from work after a long day, I don't have to put on a front for anybody. I have the breathing space to be myself.

⑨ I can wear whatever I like and not worry about what someone else thinks. I can take risks and wear things I may not have dared to wear before.

(10) I can unashamedly listen to MY kind of music whenever I want at any time of the day or night, and I can sing along at the top of my voice if I want to!

(11) I don't need validation from anyone else that I'm a good person – I can decide that for myself and be happy with my own choices and actions.

(12) I am so aware that good things are always waiting for us to just make them happen. Just when I think I might have lost my friends, my sanity, my identity, I realise I'm actually discovering them properly for the first time and building much deeper and more magical connections.

The living room was finished in the next two days.

A week later I'd done the bathroom and the kitchen. After that I moved the bed from 'our' bedroom and made the spare room 'my' bedroom. My tummy started to growl in a way that didn't need sadness as a companion but actually needed food. So I ate. I ate my favourite things with so much relish that the flavours took on a new meaning - hope.

I also started keeping a notebook by my bed and at the end of every day wrote down at least three positive things I had done that day.

✗ Went swimming...
✗ Took mam some flowers...
✗ Took the dog to the beach...
✗ Got the accounts done...
✗ Ate healthily...
✗ Bought new sofa...
✗ Didn't cry once...

I never struggled for three things. They came easily. As I wrote more and more in the book I discovered that actually, it was all to do with how I viewed things. Positive things were all around me if I only chose to notice them. And because I was writing them down I was reflecting on them. It became a beautiful way to end each day and I was keeping up with my positive days of action.

Once it was on paper and off my chest, my life didn't look too shabby.

It didn't look too shabby at all.

SOMETHING ELECTRIC_

IT WAS another stressful day at work and I was coming to the end of a week of back-breaking financial planning.

My neck ached, my back was sparking with tension and my mind felt like it was about to explode. I was overdue a break. So I was walking Dinah in the fields behind our office with Gillie when she announced she was splitting up with Marcus. I stopped in my tracks and looked at her. She looked a bit pink in the face and her eyes were glassy green, but she stood firmly and seemed calm.

"I love Marcus but we want different things. I've just been too scared to admit it."

"But why now, Gillie? What's suddenly brought this on?"

"It's been nagging away at me for ages now. And when we were doing that personal development stuff with Ben, it really got me thinking about what I want out of life. All the things I want are things Marcus refuses to commit to. I want a baby, he's not sure. I want to get married, he's not sure. I want my name on that bloody mortgage, he's not sure. Well if he's not sure after six years of being with me then he's never going to be sure is he?"

I couldn't believe I was hearing this from Gillie. I'd lost count of the times I'd mouthed off about Marcus. *Why can't he bloody well commit to her? What's wrong with him? He doesn't know how lucky he is!* I'd never understood what she saw in him. Granted, he was funny and clever, but everyone knew he never valued Gillie the way he should.

So as Gillie and I walked back to the office, we went through the action plan. She was going to go to her house now because she knew Marcus was working from home today. She was just going to come out and say it and see where it went from there.

God, this was weird. Talk about your tables turning. As she drove off and I watched her car disappear round the bend I pondered over how crazy the world was these days. Just when you thought things were stable, they crashed. Just when you thought things were solid, they melted. There was a strange energy in the air.

Something electric.

And it wasn't shifting in a hurry.

CHOICE_

Two days later we were on the second part of our business course.

Gillie and I had made it through a whole day of finance and fundraising workshops and we were still standing. Well, sitting actually - with tall gangly bloke who was now our brand new buddy, Oliver - and nattering over a coffee.

Gillie was fine. Gillie was surprisingly fine. Marcus, although a bit taken aback, had understood her reasons and just let her go. Can you believe that? He just let her go. She was slightly shell shocked and staying with me until they figured out how to go about things. She said she'd been so inspired by me and how I'd been coping that she just knew everything would be okay. So I was good for something after all. I was watching her carefully, but had to admit to a strange elation that this was the best decision she could have made.

So back to the business course. It was nearly time for the personal development part of the day so Gillie, Oliver and I supped our coffees and waited for Ben to appear. Looking round the room, I noticed lots of people had left early, muttering something about a meeting or catching a train. Strange that.

When Ben got there he clearly didn't give a flying flip about this and did that weird thing where we found ourselves in the middle of the session before we knew what was happening. No start, no ceremony. Just the sudden realisation that you are in the thick of it. He said we'd probably finish at six but I had an evening meeting, so I piped up. "Sorry Ben, I have to go to a meeting tonight and can't stay that late."

He smiled and said okay and arranged a time that suited everyone. We started talking about workloads and time management. As I was a self-certified expert in work-related stress, my ears properly perked up.

"We all have a lot of pressures at work and it's natural to struggle with that sometimes. But we can find ways to make things easier for ourselves. We could remember that the pressures we are under are quite often due to our own decision-making."

There were several snorts around the room at this point. The tiny meerkat woman who'd point-blank refused one hundred days of positive action retorted, "But there are hundreds of things I have to do every day."

Ben asked gently, "Okay, like what?"

"Well like getting my son out of bed. I have to get him off to school. I have to make the breakfast. I have to go to work."

"Okay," answered Ben. "Let's look at one thing at a time. Why do you have to get your son out of bed?"

She stared at him like he'd just dropped down from planet Zog. "Because he'd stay in bed all day if I didn't."

"So why can't you let him spend all day in bed?"

"Because he's a child! He needs to go to school."

"So, effectively, you get him out of bed in the mornings because you believe it is useful for him to get an education."

"Exactly." She sat back, arms folded, exasperated at this line of questioning.

"So you're making a choice because you want what's best

for your son." We all looked at the woman. Her shoulders softened and a smile twitched on her lips for a fraction of a second. Then she remembered where she was and stared at Ben with those beady eyes, daring him to continue.

And he did.

He turned to me.

"Jess, you said something interesting earlier. You said 'I *have* to go to a meeting tonight'. Now that phrase . . . 'I have to'. Why do you have to go to that meeting?"

I gulped. "Because it's with the local residents' association. They might be able to help us get funding for a really important project we want to do."

"Excellent. Why do you want to do that really important project?"

"Because it will raise our profile in the community, help loads of kids and families and help to sustain our company financially." I looked at Gillie. She nodded at me.

"Okay. That's great. So why do you have to raise your profile, why help loads of kids and why do you have to be sustained financially?"

"Well, because I want the community to get involved so we can show everyone how great it is to be involved in art. I want the local kids to find confidence and raise their aspirations. And I want our business to finally drag itself out of its financial mess because Gillie and I deserve to make a living out of what we believe in."

I held my breath. How could he argue with that? "That's brilliant, isn't it? That you care so much about what you do. So you could work in a different job with a steady salary and no evening meetings. But you choose this job."

"Yes." I echoed. "I choose this job." Woah. This was interesting. It's not like I didn't know it was my choice to be in this job. It was more like I'd forgotten it, probably because I'd been so busy with just plain bloody surviving over the years. It suddenly became clear that I'd been so over-worked I'd become beaten down by what seemed like everyone else's choices, everyone else's rules.

Ben went on to talk about choices. He used the analogy of sitting at home in the garden, chilling out, reading the paper / trashy magazine, drinking a cuppa / pint of wine. You are relaxed / sloshed and enjoying the tranquillity of your home. You look up and notice something is different. That tree. That lovely old tree that was at the end of your garden is gone. Your neighbour has cut it down without talking to you about it. You march inside, grab the telephone and ring him up to give him merry hell.

How dare he do this?

How dare he wreck your garden?

So obviously, everyone in the room was nodding and sympathising with the plight of the massacred tree. But Ben pointed out that, at the moment we notice the massacred tree, we have a choice. We can go mental and go and give that neighbour a piece of our mind. Or we can think of it in another way. Or better still we can actually *feel* another way. It is not the neighbour who has made us feel furious. It's not even the action of cutting down the tree. It is us. We have made ourselves feel furious.

We have chosen to be furious.

I sat back in my chair and tried to absorb this. Of course the air in the room was thick with pessimism. We were all trying to grasp what Ben was saying to us, but this hippy shit was hard to take in. It was a very beautiful thing to imagine that we could stop ourselves from feeling angry or sad or jealous or victimised at any given time, but it was quite another thing to actually feel it.

So Gillie and I gave it a trial run. On the way home we saw Oliver waiting in the rain for a bus. His usual spiky hair was so wet it was slapped across his forehead and his cheeks were apple-red with the cold. So, even though I was going to be late for my meeting, we pulled over and I shouted "Hey Oliver! We choose to give you a lift home!"

He laughed loudly into the rain. "Cheers me maties." Then he bent double and folded his massively long legs into the back of Gillie's clapped out Mini-Metro. "And I choose to accept!" He banged shut the door and off we went.

Oliver had his own business too. He was a travel photographer stuck in the world of wedding portraits to scrape together an income. He'd quite clearly seen a lot of the world so Gillie and I were always pressing him to tell stories about his experiences, but he was quietly modest and never gave that much away. He was gentle and charming and easily the nicest participant on the programme.

After we dropped Oliver outside his little stone house just outside the city, we got hopelessly stuck in heavy traffic and felt that familiar frustration starting to rise. But Gillie said "I choose to feel good about this traffic jam. I love traffic jams. Who knows what this delay will bring us!"

I copied Gillie's perky tones. "I adore traffic jams too. And I choose to cancel my bloody meeting because I am going to be too late to attend now." And with that I grabbed my mobile and made the call to reschedule the meeting. Now things were hotting up.

So Gillie took it up a level. "I choose to take the next exit off the motorway. It may take us on a longer and, frankly ridiculously long route, but we will miss the traffic and benefit from experiencing a different and hopefully invigorating drive home." By this point it was too much and I was laughing so much I could hardly get my words out.

"And I choose to turn the music up on the radio because, although I think most modern-day music is inexcusably crap, I am willing to open my mind to new and unusual sounds!"

We rolled down the windows, even though it was still raining, and laughed out loud. The music – as predicted – was inexcusably crap, but we listened anyway, driving through unknown territory and making turns at junctions based purely on blind faith. We swung curves and corners, across moors and hills and gleefully searched for familiar landmarks. The rain eventually stopped, the clouds drifted apart and revealed a bright red sun sinking slowly into the horizon.

We were headed straight for it. Straight for a blushing warmth, a cherry glow.

I finally got home after the sun had set and long after my meeting should have taken place.

I collapsed onto the sofa and a buzz settled over my body. Ben's words about choice echoed in my head. Something about when we are given a stimulus (like your neighbour chopping down a tree or an unrealistic deadline at work or – and here's a good one - your fiancé saying he doesn't love you any more), you don't just react instinctively like an animal would. No. In between stimulus and reaction we have choice. Just like we choose between a bottle of chardonnay or pinot (chardonnay every time, by the way), we choose how to feel and how to react.

I thought about Gillie and I and our newly awarded single status. She'd done a really brave thing by splitting up with a man she loved because she knew her life was on pause. That was her choice, and she had no idea where it would take her. But now she had real ownership of whatever happened afterwards. Then I thought about my reaction to Jack saying he didn't love me. I'd been a victim of his choice. He'd done that to me . . . hadn't he?

On the day we'd split up he'd offered me a solution first. A solution which meant we could stay together. But that would have involved giving up our house, our engagement and our life together all in the hope that love might save us again one day.

And what had I done? I'd said no. That's not what I want for myself. My choice. My decision.

Had I really done that? Was the split really something to do with me? It suddenly dawned on me that it was. I couldn't stay with a man who didn't love me. I couldn't give up all the things that were dear to me. I had chosen something else. I had chosen me. And, just like Gillie, I didn't know where that choice was going to take me. And now, whatever path I found myself on was mine.

I owned it.

And it looked like Gillie and I were walking that path together.

KITCHEN THERAPY_

I POURED three glasses of cheap bubbly and we swiftly chinked them together.

"Happy Birthday dad!" I said, beaming at my parents as we all gulped down our first mouthful.

Hmm. The tangy bubbles slid down my neck and I thanked the lord for twenty-four hour Tesco's. The night before I'd dashed round there at two in the morning after a hellish shift at work. I was so stressed out I'd almost forgotten it was my dad's birthday the next day and – like a fool – I'd offered to make him a special meal as a birthday present this year.

And now I was in my parents' kitchen sipping crappy champagne and chopping discount vegetables in the hope of producing something tasty. But actually it was lovely. In the midst of all the sadness and skinniness, I'd forgotten how much I enjoyed cooking and chatting with the loved ones in my life. It had always seemed like a beautiful combination.

It turned out that my mam had just received a date from the hospital for a hip replacement operation as she had arthritis that had got rapidly worse over the past year. I suddenly felt terrible for not checking on her more often and being so bloody self-obsessed. She was clearly in a lot of pain, wincing every time she tried to sit or stand or even take a few steps and I was not used to seeing her like this. Here she was in real physical pain whilst mine seemed self-invented in comparison.

We talked about the practicalities of her going into hospital and how we could keep the house running, sort out the garden, walk the dogs etc etc. I arranged to move in with dad for a while and keep things ticking over. Their house was close to my office and Gillie could look after my house and Dinah in the meantime. It was no biggie. And I could see by their faces that they'd been hoping I'd offer.

The warmth of the oven filled the kitchen and the scent of spices spiked the air as I continued cooking. With every stage in the meal's preparation, I felt calm and homely and useful. Yes useful. A bit like when I'd grabbed my notebook and made the list of why being single was 'bloody brilliant'. I felt useful to my very core as we all softened into each other's company and I could feel the sensations of smelling, tasting, drinking, listening and talking working a very particular kind of magic.

This was not a new feeling.

I'd felt it before but I had forgotten about it. I'd always loved cooking for other people, and providing a safe, warming environment for people to relax, kick back and talk about everything mundane and eventful, routine and exciting, obvious and surprising. You never knew how helpful that could be to some people. But Jack had always made it clear he didn't want people taking advantage of me. *You're too kind for your own good Jess. People are going to take the piss.*

And what I'd taken for his simple concern for me now seemed a little controlling.

So it was wonderful to reclaim that feeling on that night. I looked at my dad's rosy cheeks and even caught him squeezing my mam's hand several times, and I could feel that this was something I was good at.

It was kind of at odds with the business-woman-entrepreneur-type I seemed to spend most of my time being, but - even if just for one night - it was a warm and welcome contrast.

A BUSINESS DECISION_

THE FOLLOWING Sunday I was burning the midnight oil yet again and was racked with guilt because I'd be late back to my dad.

I was sat in my freezing cold office in a pool of stark white desk-lamp light, staring at a blur of figures on the computer screen. The next day I was starting a new project working with kids from hell in the west end of the city, trying to convince them that they would much rather be making textile banners than randomly burning cars, so I had to do the cash flow work now. It was urgent.

Figures were not my thing, but because I was company manager, it was my responsibility. So I had struggled through hours of forecasting our finances for the next two, four, six and twelve month periods so I could see if we could even afford our own salaries let alone anything else. I'd spent all day and night going through every bit of financial information I could lay my hands on.

But fuck, things were bad.

Two months on: nine thousand in the red. Four months on: sixteen thousand in the red. Six months on: thirty three thousand, and I couldn't even bring myself to look at twelve months on for fear of my eyes popping out of their sockets. I sat in that office alone, head in hands, breathing rapidly.

Oh fuck.

I closed my eyes, rubbed my brow and begged rational thought to save me. It's not like this hadn't happened before. How had I dealt with it in the past? Well, I'd call a team meeting and engineer plans to drum up emergency business. Strategic phone calls, desperate mail-outs, frantic funding bids. Somehow we always managed to weather the storm. But looking back, I could see that running this business had been storm after storm.

Did I really want to weather another one?

I leaned back in my chair and stared at the ceiling. Instead of feeling tired I actually felt really alert. My eyes were wide open and practically burning holes in the ceiling. Since the second I had started this business I had always been convinced this was what I wanted. I took pride in being the tireless business leader, the passionate community artist, the people's helper. But right now, sitting at this desk with the clock approaching midnight, something inside me wasn't so convinced anymore. I didn't feel like calling an emergency team meeting. I didn't feel like doing phone calls or mail-outs or funding bids. I didn't feel like being the tower of strength for something that was quite clearly dying on its feet.

I snapped out of my trance, printed out a copy of the deadly cash flow forecasts and shut up shop for the night.

When I got home, to my surprise, my dad was waiting up for me. He was in the kitchen warming milk on the stove. How very un-dad like.

"What are you doing up dad? You've got work in the morning."

"So have you," he said. "Honestly, Jess, I didn't realise you were still working these hours."

"Well, you know how it is."

"You look a bit hassled. Why don't you have a hot chocolate before you go to bed? I'm having one."

"Okay. But I can't stay up too late."

Ten minutes later I was sitting next to my dad on the sofa, hugging a fragrant mug and pouring my heart out about the business. I didn't usually talk to my dad about this type of stuff but hey, nothing was normal these days.

"And the thing is dad, there just seems to be no way out of it. We've tried for years to find funding to keep ourselves going but it's not out there. We always end back up at this place where I'm sat with my head in my hands on a Sunday night trying to think of ways to survive. When will it all end?"

"Well it might not end, Jess. Maybe this is the way it is."

God, he was so right. "When I was with Jack I didn't care, because whenever it looked bad I always had him to fall back on. I never minded having no life outside of work because he was my life and we worked together. But now the equation doesn't add up. I still believe in the business, I've never stopped believing in what we do. But now *my* life is being compromised for it. I hate to say it but I don't want to compromise the quality of my life."

I sank into the sofa because I knew the inevitability of what I was saying. Dad patted my arm.

"It's okay love. There is no shame in what you're saying."

I blinked back the tears. "But I just feel so awful about it! I'm the leader of Firebelly. Gillie relies on me. Loads of kids and their parents rely on me. I can't stop doing it, I would let so many people down."

"But you're letting yourself down by not doing what *you* need to do," Dad said. "Remember when you used to do all that writing? When was the last time you wrote something just for the hell of it? Come to think of it, when was the last time you had a day off or a holiday or when did you last do absolutely nothing?"

Well, I couldn't even answer these questions because I didn't want to hear myself say the words. So the tears took over instead and my dad hugged me tight as he witnessed me sobbing for the fifty billionth time that year. But he knew this was years' worth of strain finally coming out of me. As my dad, I think he knew it better than I did.

I felt a distant relief because this wasn't even about Jack. This was about me and what I wanted. I had no way of knowing what would happen to me in the future, but I did know that as long as I ran this business, it would always have to come first. And maybe – just maybe – I wanted to put me first instead.

———

The next day I was in the middle of fabric painting with those kids from hell, successfully distracting them from burning my car, when I called Gillie to see if she could come round to my parents' house that night.

When she came round we went out into the garden and drank tea in the mild evening shade. My dad knew why I'd asked her round and made himself scarce. I had no idea how to start this with her. It felt like I'd cheated on my own best friend. So I started by showing her the cash flow forecast. She paled. I took a deep breath. "Gillie, I'm not sure we should keep doing this."

She looked up at me, wide eyed. "What do you mean?"

I asked Gillie to remember one of the exercises we had done with Ben. It was just a simple thing where he gave us all a blank sheet of paper and asked us to write down things we wanted to fill our lives with. I hadn't thought much of it at the time, but when I'd looked at mine again, I took more notice at what I had written: painting, long weekends, writing, dancing, going to the pub, travelling, spending time with friends and family, cooking, helping people, reading, yoga, children, walks on the beach, talking, listening. Incidentally, there was nothing about filling my days with being skinny, which was encouraging. And the closest thing to work or any kind of career was: being financially independent. That's it. Nothing more.

"And when I looked at the list Gillie, I started to think that maybe it was possible to fill my life with all of those things. Why should they be just for other people like I've always imagined? Rich people, lazy people, lucky people. They could be for me. But they will never be for me – or you – as long as we have Firebelly."

Gillie and I talked into the night. She was a bit shocked that I was even going there in my head but the issues were familiar to her too. So we decided. Then and there in my parents' little garden with the scent of my mam's herb garden pinpricking the air and the coolness of the evening making us shiver. We would end the business. We would each start something new. God knows what but it would be new.

Bloody hell. Jess without a business. Jess without a Jack.

Was the earth actually still turning?

KATY_

Gillie and I knew we had to act quickly before we lost our nerve.

And just as you would plan a business start-up carefully, you would do the same with a business shut-down.

The first task was to speak to our new recruit, Nicola. It was not easy, especially as we'd only just taken her on. But she totally took the news on the chin. Most of all she was sorry she wouldn't be able to work with us anymore, but generally she understood how it had come to this. Phew.

Secondly, we needed to speak to our guidance committee so we called a meeting. As they arrived one by one, I busied myself with the usual job of stapling agendas, making coffees and handing out biscuits. After a few minutes everyone was there, sitting round the table, curiosity all over their faces, and Gillie looked nervously in my direction. Okay then. Over to me.

First I showed everyone the cash flow scenario. This was met with loads of questions about how on earth it had got so bad, what could be done to avoid it and was it a case of bad cash flow or an unviable business? This led me conveniently – but excruciatingly – on to our decision to close down. "And so, Gillie and I have decided to close Firebelly and move on to our own ventures. Nicola knows all about it. The shut-down should take about six months." I shuffled my papers into a stunned silence.

It was torturous. But after a while Gillie rescued me. The meeting turned into less of a formality and more of a heart-to-heart discussion. Once the initial shock had worn off and people started to see why the decision had been made, I parachuted back down to earth and eased myself into the flow of things.

It felt so bloody weird to be having this conversation. We'd built Firebelly from absolutely nothing. And whilst it had been built on stamina, motivation, practicality and sense, its foundations were also firmly rooted in love, belief and carefully chosen values. It was the only career I had ever wanted.

And now I was chucking it all away.

But I was also chucking away stress and pressure. I was chucking away sleepless nights and stupid deadlines. This process of shutting down would be long and emotional – especially considering there was a ten grand overdraft to deal with first – but this was the right choice for me. And Gillie.

By the end of the meeting, things felt sad and odd. Having stuck with us through the years, people could appreciate that Firebelly had become too much of a burden, but they were also saddened that this was the end.

We planned to shut down by the end of October. With the work commitments already in the diary and by bagging a few other projects, we should be able to finish the bank balance at zero without any debts for Gillie and I to pay. Just.

As everyone was gathering their things and I was busy washing up some mugs in the sink, the chairperson came to say goodbye.

"Well done Jess, that can't have been easy. Especially considering what that bastard Jack has done to you."

I looked at her. The mention of Jack made my stomach flip but I said, "He's not a bastard. It just wasn't working."

"Well, I'd be calling him every name under the sun if it was me. Can't believe he's moved in with that Katy already."

I dropped a mug in the sink. It clanged. "Katy?"

"Yeah, you know, that Katy bird from the pub. You did know, didn't you?"

"Yes. Of course I did." She mumbled something else. Gillie took her to one side. I stared into the sink. People tucked in chairs, zipped bags, said goodbyes, closed doors.

Cars drove off, water kept running, hands still soapy, eyes still staring, heart stopped.

Katy.

TURKEY_

I think Gillie shook me.

I think she tried to hug me. I think she talked at me, shouted at me and pleaded me to say or do something.

I think I threw something. I think I sat on the floor. I think Gillie picked me up and walked me to a chair. I think I cried because when I finally snapped out of it my cheeks were wet and my eyes were stinging.

Katy.

I knew her. She owned the very pub that Jack and I had been at on New Year's Eve, the night it all kicked off. The very pub Jack worked at now. The very pub Jack and I had spent countless nights in over the last few years. She was curvy and pretty, she was tomboyish and jolly. She was nice. Emphasis on the 'was'.

Gillie said, "Maybe they're not actually together. You heard. He's just moved in there. He's got a job there hasn't he? Maybe it's just for convenience."

Yeah, very convenient. Of course they were together. Every time we used to go to the pub she would buy us both drinks, slap us on the backs, flash us smiles with her beer-reddened cheeks. Well at least now I knew why. For God's sake, the weekend before I even knew anything was wrong with us, he'd gone out on the town without me and stayed at the pub overnight! How could I have been so stupid? I'd said go on Jack, you enjoy yourself Jack, you stay out as long as you want Jack, you shack up with whoever you bloody well like Jack.

How stupid could I possibly be?

While Gillie drove me home, I thought this is it.

This is the thing I've been waiting for. The pain was almost victorious because I knew all along it had been coming. Images of them played in my head like a forbidden film and I thought I might be violently sick. Jack was with someone else. Only a few months on and Jack was with someone else.

How long had they been together? Could he have been with her before he finished with me? How could he think so little of our relationship to move on so quickly? How the hell could he actually move in with her and leave me to be the laughing stock of the entire world? Who the hell did he think he was? Shacked up in his little love nest with beer and fags and sex on tap. Oh god. He was having sex with her. How could he? Didn't he know the rule was to never contemplate sex ever again. At least, not until I was married and settled with fifty seven children.

In my 'Three Positive Things' book that night I wrote:

1. Didn't Kill Jack
2. Didn't Kill Katy
3. Didn't kill self.

The following days continued in the same vein.

No murders, no suicides.

But not much else. Work, dog walking, work, dog walking. Oh, and constant meal avoidance. This felt familiar. This felt distinctly like Square One. My friends started looking at me in that 'we-know-she's-devastated-but-when-is-she-going-to-buck-herself-up' kind of a way. Closing the business became a minor detail and Jack And His New Girlfriend became my new project. Poor Gillie. She was on her own for a while, watching me shuffle through my work commitments and just waiting for me to be ready to deal with things again. But I didn't know if I wanted to be ready.

The pain was something I knew how to live with, like an old friend I could welcome in with open, weary arms.

One thing to be grateful for was that my mam's operation had gone well. I hadn't enjoyed seeing her looking all frail and thin, resting on the hospital bed like a piece of fine paper blown in by a breeze. But gradually she was regaining her strength and eventually arrived back home with special support cushions and walking sticks a plenty. I moved back to my house at my parents' insistence but made sure I checked on them every day.

Even if it was all done with a face like a slapped arse.

One day, Gillie came home after a business course day. I didn't go because I couldn't face the idea of personal development when I was having problems developing basic speech let alone myself. Gillie said Oliver was asking after me and then chattered about the kind of stuff they'd done. She unrolled a big sheet of paper and showed me a collage she'd made out of pictures from magazines. "It's my vision sheet." She said proudly. It shows things I want to achieve over the next three years." Gillie bounded through to the sitting room, and asked if she could borrow glue and scissors. She wanted to finish her sheet.

I watched her chopping and cutting and gluing. I put on some music for her so she could really enjoy her work. After a while it was too much and I had to join in. It was either that or brood in the kitchen over my seventy-eighth cup of tea.

Before long my vision sheet was taking shape. I'd rifled through magazines just grabbing the images that appealed to me, actively avoiding all of the unspeakably thin models because I knew in my heart of hearts that they had no place in my vision for my future self. This was a brave act in itself and made me feel that a meaningful, helpful self-awareness could slink back in if I only let it. Collages of colours and patterns, the ocean, sunsets, sunrises, mountains, mothers and babies, bare feet in the sand, cafés, books, paints and globes. I leaned back and looked at my work. So this was me on a page. And again, nothing really connected with my career. Nothing really connected with money.

And, now that you mention it, nothing really connected with Jack. God, wouldn't it be amazing if I could achieve a life like this?

The phone rang.

Gillie jumped to answer it and I took my work through to the kitchen to make another cuppa. I watched the kettle rattle and boil and looked at my collage. I felt a bit calmer. I felt a bit more human. Funny how a bit of glue and paper can help stick you back together.

As I was pouring the tea Gillie skidded into the kitchen.

"Oh my god, Jess, you're never going to guess what. That was Ella on the phone. She can get hold of some cheap flight tickets and has invited us and Vicky to go on a week's holiday with her. It's next week. Do you want to go? Do you want to go? Do you want to go?"

My first reaction was yes. But then I remembered my life here. I remembered Jack and his new bit of fluff and my heart thudded. How could I summon the energy to go on holiday when I was needed here to stomp and glare and brood? I dropped my eyes but caught in my gaze was my vision sheet. Full of loveliness and gorgeous stuff and my identity on a page.

And so it tumbled out of my mouth, "Yes. I want to go."

"Woo hoo!" Gillie yelped and hugged me tightly, squashing my head in the process. "The only thing is, we have to decide, Portugal or Turkey?"

"God, I don't know. Turkey!" I'd been to Portugal as a kid and fancied something completely new. Turkey was not somewhere I'd considered before, but hey, why not? Gillie skipped back into the living room to call Ella and Vicky and get it all sorted.

Bloody hell, a girlie holiday. I'd never been on one before. It would mean deserting the business for a whole week. Not something I would have even dreamt of six months ago, but suddenly it all seemed very possible. Gillie and I would look at our work commitments and either re-shuffle them or get other artists in to do the work in our absence.

And do you know what?

That's exactly what we did.

IPEKLIKUM_

THE FOUR OF us arrived in Ipeklikum, meaning 'Silken Sands', in the dead of night.

We were greeted at our apartment complex by a young lad called Hakan who looked incredibly exotic but as soon as he opened his gob out came a thick cockney accent, "Alright gals? I believe you're on the top floor. Look lively, let's go." He rattled open the door, dumped our suitcases in the porch and chucked our keys on top.

"'Ome sweet 'ome." He grinned and off he went.

This was good.

We'd totally landed on our feet.

The apartment was clean, modern, bright, airy. Bless Ella and her magical ticket-acquiring abilities. After the inspection we gathered outside on the darkened balcony, linked arms and breathed in the night air. We could hear nothing but the breeze rustling the tall grasses, and crickets chirping sleepily and as we looked at each other with broadening smiles, we all knew this had been a very, very good idea.

The first couple of days were most definitely pool days.

We would flip flop down the stairs, set up camp on four parallel sun beds, leaf through girlie mags and sigh into the sun. It wasn't much of a surprise that I had a pretty awful and debilitating bikini-confidence-crisis at first and spent a lot of time clad in good old kaftans. I gazed at Gillie's strong curvy lines in a glamorously beaded, white bikini; Ella splashing about in her striped surf shorts and cropped swimming top; Vicky with her small but perfectly formed hips skimmed by an orange-glow sarong and her ample bosom packaged into a fiery bikini top. And there was me. Skinnier than usual, yes, but all white skin and sticky-out elbows, an oil-drum waist and unwanted fatty dimples. But after a while I got my personal development head on and thought, *what the hell am I worrying about? Nobody gives a shit about my dimples and flaws. What, does the earth revolve around me?* And so came the discardment of the kaftans and I started strutting about in my cozzie with a real sense of 'fake it til you make it'. That would do for now, at least.

I made sure I'd packed my notebook and each night I continued recording my three positive things. I was spoiled for choice really. I mean after the whole 'I will wear a bikini and I will bloody well enjoy it' episode, things just got better.

On most evenings we would get a taxi down to the main street, find something delicious to eat and generally bask in the wonder of this place.

It was a relaxed resort, the moonlit beach living up to its silken name, daintily decorated by small restaurants and pretty little cafés, and a multitude of lanterns strung along the promenade in blushing pinks and cool blues. The resort obviously attracted people from all over the world although a small section did offer the usual Brit affair: karaokes, nightclubs and fast food places. And we were mightily impressed by the lengths the waiters would go to, to get you into their joint. We'd expected flirting and chatting – this was Turkey, after all. But we'd never expected to be treated like royalty. It was disconcerting being treated so well. I mean, we were from England, Capital of Crap Customer Service.

But it only took us a couple of nights to get into the swing of things and accept our royal service like it was our god-given right.

At our favourite restaurant, 'English Rose', there was a gaggle of gorgeous, groomed, olive skinned men, and these men really knew how to impress. It was no wonder they had the reputation they did in the rest of the world. Their routine included kissing us on the hands as we arrived; pulling out our chairs and flicking our napkins onto our laps in a single, sexy, slip of a second; making lingering eye contact over the menus; filling our glasses at every single opportunity; bringing free desserts (with extra squirty cream) and finishing the evening by crafting an elaborate rose made from a paper napkin. Was it any wonder we were hooked on this place?

There was one particular guy at English Rose, Ekrem, who had the whole routine down to an art. He was a ridiculously charming giant of a man with soft brown eyes and a broad grin, always smelling of some enticing, spicy aftershave. Watching him (and believe me, I did), you could see he was much loved by everyone, not just the women, because he really had the gift of the gab. Totally impossible for him to offend anyone's sensibilities (although I would have let him have a go at offending mine).

But the English Rose wasn't our favourite bar. We preferred 'Beerbelly', an almost secret little place hidden down an avenue leading away from the beach. It was the perfect place to either cool down after a hard day sunbathing, or to party hard into the night. Half of it was located outdoors, up some steep marble steps and gorgeously lit by little star-shaped lights hanging overhead. The other half was indoors. A kind of cool, dark cavern housing a number of rickety sofas, wicker chairs, glass-topped tables, a pool table, a gigantic TV and a mirrored bar. If you ventured right to the back of the cavern you'd find an alcove named 'Village Corner'. It was decorated with Turkish carpets, cushions and tapestries and we supposed that's where the bar boys relaxed during their very occasional time off.

The whole place was enchanting with just the right amount of rough around the edges. And it certainly wasn't lost on Gillie and I, the irony of basically replacing the 'fire' in our bellies with 'beer'. A fair swap I'd say.

Beerbelly stood right next to a tour company we'd been recommended by Cockney Hakan, called 'Mega Tour', and apparently they were joined in a mafia-type way. Mega Tour was run by Demir, who we immediately tagged as a gangster on account of his pointy shoes, stiff black suits and hair styled so rock hard it could have spiked a low-flying bird. He tried his best to be sultry but he had a real soft spot for Gillie, which ruined his hard-man image as he followed her around Beerbelly like a lost puppy.

There was one guy who kicked and scuffed about the place in his low slung, baggy shell suit (yes, shell suit). I think he was supposed to be a bar man but he preferred to stare at the floor, avoid any real work and point blank refuse to respond to any name other than 'Bad Boy'. Ironic considering he had the face of an angel. He was Demir's cousin. God knows what his real name was but we obligingly called him Bad Boy in the meantime.

Esad was the owner of Beerbelly and Demir's cousin too. He was older than the rest of them, taller and quieter and somewhat sweaty if I'm honest. He would slide up to us mid-cocktail and spout some jargon about life and souls and passions and purpose. We decided he was insane.

Then there was Mesut, who totally outstripped the rest of

them in terms of mystery. Now here was a man who knew how to do ambiguity. When you tried to talk to him he would hide behind long, dripping strands of thick black hair which hung like a curtain of privacy across his face. He was utterly bizarre and high on god knows what, but he made a mean Black Russian, so we put up with the definite feeling of unease whenever he was around.

All in all, Ipeklikum was a great place for a girlie holiday. We felt safe and welcome there. Okay so it was a bit Brits-Abroadish, but that's what we were, Brits abroad.

Having said that, by the middle of the week we decided we should really see something of Turkey while we were there. So we gatecrashed Mega Tour, made use of Demir's fascination with Gillie, and booked a heavily discounted tour to the ancient city of Ephesus. It was supposed to be one of the wonders of the world, after all.

———

It was the hottest day yet as we trailed around the massive site, marvelling at the ancient archaeological features before us.

In the ancient amphitheatre, I climbed a billion steps to the top of the auditorium, just so I could see what it looked like from up there. And for a good few minutes I just stood there, with only a warm breeze for company, allowing the moment to soak through me. I gazed down at the silvery grey stone that carved out the shape of the city and imagined what it must have been like full of people. Working people in a working city. The sounds, the smells, the tastes, the textures. The families, the feuds, the passions, the downfalls.

Demir turned up halfway through the day, claiming he'd 'forgotten' Gillie would be there on that particular tour. We had to endure him singing to her from the centre of the amphitheatre – a Kurdish love song that echoed throughout the entire acoustic marvel of the theatre and reached the ears of every other tour member there. He then spent the remainder of the day pawing – yes actually pawing at her, until she finally agreed she would go out with him the following evening.

So the next evening came and, true to her word, Gillie did go out with Demir. Only with her chaperones in tow, of course. After a few drinks at Beerbelly, we eventually ended up at a live music joint with Demir, 'Bad Boy' (shell suited, angel-faced boy), Esad (sweaty, self-certified philosopher) and Ekrem (charming, giant man from the English Rose). After a good few rounds of Raki - lethal Turkish drink, equivalent of Greek Ouzo - we all headed for the moonlit beach.

I remember that beach so well. It was the way it came alive at night. There were groups of people circled round camp fires, singing, humming or swaying to tunes being played on a guitar or a Turkish saz. There were couples huddled together, whispering and kissing in the lilac moonlight. There were families dipping their toes into the cool, black water. Children stomping in the sand and revelling at the idea of being up so late. And then there was us. Sitting round a single tealight, drinking Turkish beer and leaning back to look up at the stars.

So what if we were repeating an endless pattern of English girls meet Turkish boys? We didn't care. Even I didn't care and that's saying something. Here I was in a foreign country feeling confident, relaxed and sexy. Yes, sexy. Bloody hell, it had been a million years since I'd felt like that. But thanks to an overdose of moonlight, raki and advances from a range of pretty damn gorgeous men, I was going to bloody well enjoy the feeling.

Ekrem, in particular, was coming on strong. His English was outstanding and he was clearly practised at all of this. But that didn't bother me. I was warming to him by the second, so when he asked me to go for a walk along the beach with him, I knew my answer would be yes.

We strolled along and as he spoke I felt his hand fall to my waist. It felt good. Naughty, but good. I knew exactly where this was going and I just had to decide whether or not I was up for it. As we reached the end of the beach, we climbed up some rocks and over a railing onto a balcony of a posh hotel. "Let me, I help you," he said and pulled me up as if I was as light as a supermodel. Smooth. He'd obviously done this before.

We sat close together under the silvery shade of the balcony. A little bit of small talk. A little bit of silence. I joked with him "So Ekrem, do you come here often?"

He laughed awkwardly, my genius joke lost on him. Then he looked at me so intensely my only instinct was to laugh out loud. And then I kissed him. Full and hard on the lips, I kissed him. When I pulled back he hardly gave me two seconds to breathe before kissing me again. This time fast, purposeful and strong. I have to admit, although his kissing was a little speedy, it felt good to be in his hands. He was a big man and his arms, his hands, his frame, swallowed me up into a gorgeous sense of fire and femininity. After a few moments, we found a pace of kissing that worked for both of us and I really started to enjoy myself. It was delicious to be with this man.

This foreign, alien, stranger of a man, who knew nothing about me. He just folded me up in a blissful, lustful ignorance and took me into the heat of the unknown.

The heat of the unknown involved an incredibly uncomfortable plastic sun bed, clammy, moonlit skin, and a condom grabbed out of my bag at the (very) last minute. But ultimately it was good. So ridiculously good. We laughed afterwards at the terrible cliché we were. All flushed cheeks and racing pulses. Messy hair and misplaced underwear. What a night.

When we walked along the beach to join the others, we kicked water at each other in a pathetic attempt to blame our dishevelled appearance on fun fighting. I could feel Gillie's eyes on me before she even came into view.

When I got back to the apartment with her that night she half screamed, half whispered, "You didn't sleep with him, did you?"

I buried my head into my pillow and spoke into it, something resembling the word 'yes'. Gillie squealed and insisted on knowing every tiny detail. We chattered on and on about what it had been like for me (not bad), whether I'd do it again (maybe), what his technique had been like (so so) and whether I'd thought about Jack (not really). We decided that all in all it had been a hell of a thing to do and definitely time to cross 'have a holiday fling' off the old bucket list. And as our words slowed to a murmur and our eyes closed drowsily, sleep finally came over me. A sweet sleep, of satisfaction and dreamy amusement.

The rest of the holiday featured equal measures of hilarity, heat and headiness. I saw Ekrem another couple of times and spent a final, gorgeously naked afternoon with him in his flat on my last day. Bearing in mind it had been a lifetime since I'd been with anyone other than Jack, I was quite surprised at my own prowess. There was something liberating about being with a man I knew I was never going to see again. He was a nice man too – totally harmless and very upfront about the bizarre world he was a part of. He didn't pretend for a second that I was special or different. I was just one of many and I loved the anonymity of it.

It freed me in a way that I didn't expect from an encounter with a man. So it was welcome.

After my last afternoon with Ekrem I found a sunny spot in Beerbelly bar, where I had arranged to meet the girls. I ordered my final cocktail from a brooding Mesut, avoided Bad Boy's glares and sat at my table to watch the world go by. The late afternoon sun was dropping in the sky and melting lazily into the sea. I tried to lap up my final moments in this place. If I closed my eyes I could hear the sea rolling quietly on the sand, music floating from a number of places and beats clashing softly out of time. My limbs were loose and droopy, my mind calm and still.

Remember this feeling Jess. Remember it well.

The girls arrived and we spent the last hour reminiscing about the week's events, laughing out loud about the people and places we'd experienced. That week I had half forgotten who I was and it wasn't until we were sitting on that plane back home that I remembered what was in store for me back in England. A queasy coldness settled over me. Ah my old friend panic.

For a moment there I thought you'd left me.

"So that was the first time you came here? To Ipeklikum?" Lindy asked. "And you've obviously been home since. I'm assuming you didn't jump off the plane, do a runner back to the nearest bar and you're not currently shacked up with that Ekrem bloke."

Jess giggled. "Tempting, but no, I did actually go home. You can't live in holiday land forever."

"Shame really," Lindy said. "Then you wouldn't have had to face up to all that business stuff and deal with Katy and Jack."

"Well, let's look at it this way: everything I had to deal with when I got home was a result of my own shit." She shrugged. "You make your bed, you lie in it."

"Really? Come on. You had it pretty rough since last new year's eve. Your fiance ran out on you, your business fell apart, your mum was ill and in hospital."

"Okay, let's see." Jess started ticking things off on her fingers. "My fiance didn't love me anymore. True. But he left pretty much because I told him to, because I wasn't willing to compromise my values. My business didn't fall apart, I spent years building an ultimately unviable model and the time came when I just had to admit that. And my mam, well her illness didn't happen to me – it happened to her. I just had to decide to be there for her and my dad, no matter what was going on with me. You see?"

"Kind of," Lindy said. As far as she was concerned, it took an immense swallowing of pride to take responsibility in that way. She wasn't sure she wanted to be that grown up. Where was the fun in it? Although, looking at Jess now, who was currently drawing patterns in the sand with her toes, she didn't seem to be burdened by it. She had a sense of fun about her that was infectious and a way of seeing the world that intrigued Lindy. And god knew she hadn't been anywhere near intrigued in a very long time.

"So what was the holiday all about? If it wasn't about escaping from all the fuckery that was happening?"

"Oh, it was definitely about escaping," Jess said, looking up from her sand doodles. "You couldn't get me out of there quick enough once I'd decided to do it. There's that old cliche that a change is as good as a rest and it's bloody well true. That holiday really did do me the world of good. It created a sense of space around all of the 'fuckery.' It was simple and uncomplicated and warm and freeing and all the things a good holiday should be."

"But?"

"But real life was still there, waiting in the wings. The holiday was just a survival tactic."

And with those words from Jess, Lindy realised that that was exactly what *she* was doing here now, in Ipeklikum.

This was *her* survival tactic.

She'd agreed to come with her mum and dad as an escape route, yes, but if she'd stayed back at home a second longer things would just have got ugly. So, she realised with a delicious degree of relief, that maybe she did have a bit of insight into herself. That maybe she had made the right decision and this weird jaunt out to the Turkish coast in the depths of winter might actually prove to be a precious pause.

Had Lindy, by taking the only fathomable choice that seemed available at the time, actually gone and created a situation for herself that would ultimately increase her choices?

Stranger things had happened.

ALMOST LIKE MEMORIES_

THE HOLIDAY BLUES set in good and proper.

I'd returned home to a to-do list which included the ever-so-slightly life changing tasks of a.) closing life-long, passion-fuelled business and b.) signing official separation papers with ex-fiancé.

Nice.

But there was something amid the chaos of this that allowed me time out to breathe. The holiday had done me good. The holiday had got me smiling. The holiday had got me laughing, joking, relaxing and – who'd have thought it – even shagging again. The holiday had helped me remember the importance of being still sometimes, and re-introduced me to a confidence that only comes your way if you allow it.

So whilst I set about my epic to-do list, I kept getting distracted by this strange, distant feeling. I can only describe it as a sense of calm that prickled the senses and somehow found its way in, to the extent that I kept giving myself little breaks to accommodate it. Occasional cups of tea. Random walks. Lunchtime swims. Strange, staring-into-space type moments.

And they all felt lovely. They all felt essential.

Because this year hadn't exactly been filled with these kinds of moments so far, I struggled to compare them with any recent feelings. But the one feeling I could single out was that time I'd cooked a meal for my dad's birthday. Something that came from that wonderful mixture of listening, talking, cooking and tasting. And I think, whilst I'd been on holiday, I'd got a similar feeling from the mixture of sea, friends, warmth and laughter. These strange zombie episodes (as Gillie liked to call them) were kind of cool. Almost like memories. If I hadn't known better I would have said a memory was coming back to me.

But I did know better. So I just got on with that dreaded to-do list, allowing myself time out whenever I could.

With the exception of our guidance committee, Gillie and I still hadn't told anyone we were closing the business. But right now we were slap-bang in the middle of summer holiday projects with jumped-up, hard-done-to kids and there wasn't really much time to come up with an exit strategy. Still, we'd done the hardest part by actually making the decision, and were happy to start the ball rolling in a few weeks when the summer was over.

There was someone we needed to tell though. The people who ran the business development course. It was kind of ironic that we'd signed up to this course so that we could move the business forward, and less than halfway through we'd decided to jack it all in. We wouldn't be their finest success story, now would we?

When I called them, I got through to a Dave and whilst I'd expected him to tell me to piss right off, I was surprised to find him insisting that we finish the course. "We can help you with this stuff Jess. You and Gillie don't need to do it alone, it's what we're here for."

And before I knew it, we had experts helping us with final cash flows, stock-takes and announcement plans. Suddenly everything seemed a bit less scary. It was as if these people had come along and answered our prayers – supporting us all the way and making one of the most difficult decisions of our life a little easier. We were actually going to make this happen. Firebelly was really going to end and we were really going to have to find something else to do. And I had no fucking clue where to start with that.

So, in the same life-altering, table-turning, totally surreal way, I met up with Jack.

In some place in my brain I'd been expecting him to look different. I don't know why. I think it was something to do with him having a new girlfriend. Perhaps he'd be wearing different clothes. Perhaps he'd have a new haircut. Perhaps he'd look guilty. Perhaps he'd be smothered in bright red lipstick and be wearing a giant sandwich board splattered with the words: "I am Katy's now."

But no, of course, he looked just the same. Like my Jack. Like my old, gorgeous, brilliant Jack.

The two of us sat in the solicitor's office sitting adequately far apart and nodding at the solicitor's every word. I don't think either of us understood what we were signing apart from the facts that no, we weren't together anymore, yes, the house now belonged to me and, great, it was costing us seven hundred pounds. Or rather it was costing me seven hundred pounds. Jack was as skint as ever and needed to borrow his share of the fee until he could afford to pay me back.

Some things never change.

As I drove Jack to the centre of town afterwards, the car hissed with an uneasy silence. I stared hard at the road in front, hoping that would excuse me from actually having to speak and willed him to say something like, *don't worry babe, she's not a patch on you*. But there was nothing of the sort. I couldn't believe he could be so downright ignorant to assume I would loan him the solicitor's fees in one breath and blatantly ignore the matter in hand in another. Arrogant sod.

Just as I was about to drop him off, Jack stretched out his legs into the footwell of the passenger side, casually laced his hands behind his head and flicked his eyes my way. He yawned dramatically and at the end of the long breath out, the words almost slurred out. "I'm presuming you've heard the news through the grapevine?" I continued staring at the road ahead, wondering where one gets a grapevine these days, with which to strangle one's ex.

"You know, that I'm with someone new now." Someone new? Someone new? How old was he? Twelve? Had he picked out the new girl in the fucking playground or what?

"It's just that . . . well . . . yeah, I thought you would probably already know. So, all sorted then?" His voice tilted hopefully, like a toddler whining for ice cream and I realised he wanted some kind of approval.

What a bloody cheek. Well, he wasn't going to get it. He wasn't going to get a single thing from me. You make a choice, you live with it Jack, regardless of how other people see it.

So without a word I chucked him out action movie style, barely even bringing the car to a stop. What did I care if he got run over? He had *someone new* to tend to his needs now. I was young and free and independent don't you know? I was living one hundred days of positive action and I knew all about choices.

And after ten minutes I was also crying my heart out.

I rang Gillie.

She sighed, "Stay there Jess. I'm coming."

OLIVER_

THE NEXT DAY I tried taking my work outside of the office to a little café overlooking the river in town.

I didn't have any project work and I'd spent all morning up to my neck in financial exit strategies. Naturally my head now felt like it was about to implode. The possibility of ending this business debt-free was looking unlikely and it made me feel sick to think that Gillie and I might have to miraculously find a few thousand pounds when we should be going out on a high.

How the hell were we supposed to do that with no jobs to go to and no particular aspirations whatsoever?

I sat in a booth in the café, my notebook open and pen poised but just couldn't find the motivation to get on with my work. I stared out of the window and saw how a weeping willow tree had slowly sagged over the water until some of its branches had plunged in and were now pulled by the flow of the rushing current. Tiny leaves tugged from their rightful places and hurried downstream chased by speckles of sunlight. Where would they end up? I blinked and rubbed my temples. Bloody hell, my head hurt. And where was that waitress with my coffee?

Just as I looked up I saw a familiar figure standing at the counter.

"Oliver!" I called, and the lanky figure snapped his head up in my direction, beamed at me and made his way over to my booth, a takeaway coffee in hand.

"Hia matey! How's tricks?" He slid into the booth opposite me and set down his coffee.

"Not too bad. How's yourself?"

"Full of beans," he said and raised his paper coffee cup as if to demonstrate. "Cheers." And at that same moment the waitress finally brought my coffee to the table. Oliver asked her to bring us two muffins. "Double chocolate. That is, if you have the time Jess?"

"For double chocolate muffins? Hell, yeah." I really couldn't refuse that face so I ignored the fact that I'd already had breakfast and swiftly pushed my papers to one side.

Oliver told me he'd nipped out to take some photos by the river, it being such a nice day. "I got some amazing snaps of that weeping willow over there. Do you see how it dips into the river? Gorgeous." I nodded and realised he was talking about the same tree I'd been obsessed by only moments before. Now his trusty camera was packaged into a rucksack by his side which he patted absentmindedly whilst he talked. He asked me what I was up to and what with the creamy coffee and the chocolate muffins and the general loveliness of the man, I told him all about our decision to close Firebelly. I knew Gillie wouldn't mind.

"Wow. Big Stuff. So what are you going to do next matey?"

"Haven't got a bloody clue. And the bank might come chasing after me for big bucks before I can go anywhere anyway."

"Hmmm. You've got help from the business course though, haven't you? You can get them to help you work out all the financial stuff. You should be concentrating on what you're going to do."

I gulped and stirred my coffee, staring down into the creamy spirals.

"You know Jess – I'm a good listener . . . and keeper of secrets. I don't know about you, but I've got all day."

I tapped the side of my coffee mug and mumbled something or other. It was a good offer. I did need to talk. But it involved Jess talking about Jess and I wasn't quite sure where to start. And why would Oliver want to listen to it all anyway? I barely knew the man. And god, I'd probably bore him to tears. But before I could change my mind, make my excuses and make the chocolate muffin a take-away Oliver chuckled softly and leaned forward.

"Don't worry Jess. Just start talking. Wherever you start it's the right place."

Honestly, I thought, *which cloud did he float down from?* And so, I began. I can't remember what I began exactly, but I began something. I think I started talking about the beginning of the year when Jack and I had suddenly gone from happiest couple in the world to complete strangers. I talked about the heartache, the lonely mornings, the empty nights, the rejection, the body issues, the pity, the suspicion, the jealousy. I talked about all the parts of myself I was disgusted with, and all the parts of myself I wished I could change. I talked about my friends and their endless patience, my family and their devoted concern, my work-life and the complex world it had become. I talked about all the stuff that I had to sort out: the house, the debts, the bank accounts, my appetite, my mam's recovery, the friendships, the dog, the ground beneath my feet.

Eventually, I sat back in defeat. Now that I'd said it all out loud, it was no wonder I was bloody knackered.

Oliver sat there. His brow smooth, chin resting on his knuckles and his body totally still. Suddenly he snapped forward with a playful smile and said "Okay. That must feel a tiny bit better, eh?" I nodded. "Mind you, you're quick to talk about your weaknesses. What about your strengths? There must be some poking about in there somewhere." He paused and it became apparent that he expected me to launch into the wonder of being me. But that didn't exactly trip off the tongue. "Okay matey. *I'm* going to tell you what your strengths are."

"That's really not necess . . ."

"From everything you've told me, and judging by the history of our friendship which spans an impressive . . . ooh . . . shall we say five hours in total? I think your strengths are," and he started ticking them off on his long, spindly fingers, "motivation, loyalty, generosity, resilience, reliability, sensitivity, consideration, energy, openness, honesty, capacity to care and without a doubt, you are very, very loving."

I shifted in my seat. Those words were fantastic, but they couldn't possibly all apply to me. I knew Oliver was waiting for me to look at him so I made a painful glance his way. "Thank you." I mumbled.

"It's not a compliment, it's an observation. Really. You have all of those things." He grinned at me and the sincerity of that smile made me smile right back at him. "So now we're onto the good stuff, have you asked yourself what you're going to do next? Like, what does Jess want now?"

That question sent shivers down my spine as I remembered Jack asking me the same question in a fit of fury during that awful, misty walk just after we'd split up. My answer then would have been Jack, Jack, Jack but I knew now that had changed.

Trouble was, I didn't know what it had changed to. "I don't know, Oliver. I suppose I need to work out what my choices are because I haven't even thought about that yet. I need to feel like I'm moving forward in a vaguely positive way."

Oliver chuckled. "Your choices, eh? You're such a swot but Ben would be proud," he said. "Anything else?"

"Erm . . . well . . . God, I just want to feel a bit more secure."

"Meaning?"

"If I could just find a sense of place in myself, you know? And I need to stop sliding up and down this crazy scale between insanity and rationality. The highs and the lows have been ludicrous. It's bloody knackering!"

He smiled. "That's good, really good. What are you doing?"

"Hang on a sec. Just need to write some of this down." As I'd been talking some weird force had urged me to pick up my discarded notebook and pen and start making notes about what I was saying. I mean, I was saying stuff out loud that was really important. I didn't want to forget a single word of it . . .

CHOICES ... SECURITY ...SENSE OF PLACE

Oliver beamed and said, "Okay, now we're cooking on gas. I get a sense this is more like you. Keep that pen in your hand matey. So tell me, what things do you need to aim for now? Maybe think of three to start off with?"

I didn't think too hard. I just started scribbling as soon as the words came into my head.

HAPPY ... SECURE ... CONFIDENT

I swivelled the notebook round so Oliver could see. "Sounds good to me. But how will you know if you get there? What do those things look and feel like?"

Good question, I thought. It's all very well knowing that's what I want but how would I know I finally had them? What would be the sensations? I thought about each one separately and made doodles and scribbles as I talked to Oliver. Somehow it helped me feel more in tune with an inner voice that might actually be mine.

"Well, for happiness I really think it would be belly laughing. You know the kind I mean. The deep, genuine kind of laughing that seems to pour out of you when you're a kid. The kind that blots out everything else and you get swallowed up in it. I'll know I'm really happy when I start to belly laugh again." Oliver was about to say something but I interrupted with my next thought which just snapped up of nowhere. "And I'll start to have that smile again!"

"*That* smile?"

"It's hard to explain but people have pointed it out loads of times before. I haven't got a clue what it looks like but I know what it feels like."

"And?"

"It feels warm . . . and easy . . . and properly spontaneous."

"It sounds fab! So can you remember times when you've had this smile?" Oliver asked and eyed my notebook with enthusiasm.

That was it. Pen in hand I chattered on about *that* smile whilst I poured my thoughts onto the pages. Suddenly it felt like we were talking about the most important topic in the world.

★Starting Firebelly ... EVERYTHING possible...
Smiles on kids' faces & creativity in the air!

★Valentine's Day... Marcus in the cafe...
the sparkle in my eye

★Dad's birthday... Cooking in the kitchen...
talking and soothing and calming

"Yeah, that's totally it Oliver. One day, when I'm proper happy, I'll have that smile all the fucking time!"

"Can't wait to see it." He mused. "Okay, so that's 'happy' taken care of. What about 'secure'? What will that feel like?"

"I'm not sure if I've ever felt completely secure so it's a tough one . . . but . . . well, it would be regardless of the place I was in. It would be inside me." I started sketching out shapes in my notebook. Tunnels and circles and spheres and in all of them I was imagining how the centre would feel. Warm, cosy, secure. Then words flew off the end of my pen:

✶ <u>Secure</u> in my friendships, my family, my connections with others...

✶ Still and at ease with myself.... HAPPy with my own company

✶ <u>REVEL</u> in the unknown...

✶ Find home wherever I am because my security is inside me, <u>not</u> inside bricks & mortar...

Then we were onto 'confidence' which is where I got hopelessly stuck. Oliver suggested, "Maybe it's because you don't know what true confidence feels like. But wouldn't you like to? How would you recognise it if it came banging at your door?"

"Well, I wouldn't be comparing myself to other people all the bloody time." I was embarrassed about admitting this out loud but something told me I could trust Oliver with it. "I would love other people's attributes unconditionally instead of wishing I could be as good or as cool or as skinny or as beautiful. And I wouldn't be afraid to let them know about it. I would love my own strengths and weaknesses and I would learn from them every day. I wouldn't need to find things to fill emotional gaps . . . " In my book I noted:

" . . . because I would be full of inner strength and I would try new things whether I felt fear or desire – it wouldn't matter."

By this point I was not only surprised at my own fluency on the topic, but I was also feeling flipping brilliant. I could really speak freely because Oliver didn't have any hopes or expectations for me, he just wanted to listen. A delicious energy shot down my spine. Almost as soon as I felt this Oliver stood straight up.

"Let's go for a walk. We can keep chatting as we go."

So we walked along the banks of the river in the shifting light of the afternoon sun. We chatted about other stuff but kept coming back to the things I'd been exploring in the café. I was curious about what Oliver was doing with me. His manner, his language, his philosophies, it all intrigued me. "How do you know all this stuff anyway, Oliver? Why do I suddenly feel like I've got my own personal life coach?"

He laughed. "I don't really know any more than you Jess. It's just that, with me, it's probably a bit less buried."

I had a fleeting suspicion that I might be in the company of a total loon, or perhaps an undiscovered genius. But I had to admit that there it was again - that strange feeling of a distant memory. Had I been interested in this stuff before? Because there was something about it that felt familiar. I'd always claimed to be in tune with alternative ways of thinking and being and healing and all that jazz but had I ever actually felt it?

Really *felt* it so I could actually believe it?

We found a little wooden bench out on a quiet back street near the river. The street was deserted and all we could hear were the sounds of the river running smoothly by. Oliver took out his camera and started taking shots of the cobbled street which was striped with deep purple shade and glimmering white light reflected by the moving water. I sat on the bench and watched him. He crouched and bent and stretched and twisted to get the shots he wanted and after a while he plonked himself next to me on the bench.

I thought, *now there's a man in his element.*

We sat face to face. "Okay Jess. This might sound weird but hell, just go with it, okay? Now sit comfortably, relaxed. If it feels alright for you, just close your eyes."

I shot him a vaguely suspicious look but he looked so open and honest I just didn't have the heart to distrust him. So I did as he said. My palms were turned upwards and my shoulders dropped. We sat in silence for a few moments. Soft breeze. Church bells. Cool shade.

"So while you've got your eyes closed and you're sitting on this bench, have a think about the kind of happiness you've been talking about today. Think about that amazing smile you mentioned. Remember? Now, really imagine what it feels like when you've got that smile on your face. If it helps, remember a time when somebody pointed it out to you and imagine all the feelings that went with that. Have you got it matey?"

"Yes," I murmured. I was imagining me in my denim dress on Valentine's Day. Marcus commenting on how I seemed. The sparkle in my eye. The smile on my lips. The flooding warmth that moment gave me.

"Now imagine that feeling, that smile, starting in the centre of you. Then it takes over your body and your insides. Just let it wash over you and fill you up. Is it warm or cold? Is it soft or hard? If that feeling was a colour, what would it be?"

"Orangey-yellow."

"Great. Orangey-yellow. Just let that colour fill the memory of the moment and be completely in it. Allow yourself to feel this good. It's your feeling."

Oliver stayed quiet for a while now. I was in my lovely orangey-yellow land of confidence. It was amazing how I could capture the power *that* smile gave me. As I was sat there on the bench, in the deserted street, opposite Oliver, I really did feel a happiness. Maybe only for a few moments. But I did feel it.

When I opened my eyes I realised I was smiling. A bloody big one too. Oliver laughed out loud and said "That's it. That's the one." And of course that just caused it to broaden even more and I could have cried from it. I could have cried from the smile that freed me so perfectly.

But instead I whipped out my notebook and scrawled in huge letters:

Practice THAT Smile!!!

"Thanks Oliver, that was amazing."

"Yeah. It's just a simple meditation but it works wonders. And you can do it any time now. Shall we walk?"

We turned and walked slowly up the winding streets and back into the city centre. Back to people and cars and noise and traffic jams. Since we'd met in the café, four hours had passed, but it had felt like five minutes. I was buzzing with energy. "Thanks again Oliver. I'm so chuffed I bumped into you."

"No probs, matey. I'm pleased I bumped into you too. You've got loads of stuff racing around in my head too – values, beliefs, and all that hardcore life stuff. Speaking of which, I'm off to work some photographic magic on the church now but I'll see you around soon, okay?"

"Okay."

Oliver merged into the flowing rush-hour crowd and I headed in the direction of my car. But then I heard him shout "Jess!" and I snapped round to see him making weird signs with his hands and mouthing something enthusiastically. *What the hell is he doing?* I thought. But after a couple of repetitions, I realised he was mouthing the word "notebook" and tracing the shape of it with his fingers. He was telling me to keep using it.

I stuck my thumb up in the air to show him I understood perfectly and assure him that yes, I would be using my notebook more often from now on.

And I meant it.

I was back at home.

I'd returned an hour or so earlier high on energy from my chance meeting with Oliver. I was feeling so bloody great I'd practically skipped round the fields with Dinah, the both of us revelling in the fresh air and the muddy puddles. Now she was in the kitchen scoffing a bowl of stinky dog food and I had purposefully shunned the TV for my notebook. I was in my bedroom and was lying on my belly on my bed, legs kicked upwards and pen poised.

I traced over the letters as I thought about those words.

It was something Oliver had said as he'd left me: *You've got loads of stuff racing around in my head too – values, beliefs, and all that type of hardcore life stuff.* How the hell I'd managed to help him do anything whilst he had practically become my guardian angel for the day, I don't know, but he'd said it all the same. And the words had got stuck in my mind. 'Values' and 'Beliefs'. They certainly sounded like something I should have, and something I should be certain about. Something I should perhaps wear on a t-shirt or paint on a banner or start a hippy protest about. But what the hell were they anyway? And why didn't I know what mine were?

Okay, one at a time:

Maybe if I could work out what my values were, I could understand myself better. Okay, so fill a page Jess. Fill a page with your values.

Right.

There. Job done.

I looked at the words I'd written and realised how easy it was to come up with values. They were just things that had been important to me ever since I could remember and helped to make up my character.

And I thought they were all fairly honourable and respectable.

I flipped over onto my back and held my notebook above me, looking again at what I'd written. Hang on a minute. Honourable and respectable to who? Where was I on the page? None of those things actually related to me. As I read each word I could see that what I'd done was write about my relationships with the rest of the world. Nothing on there was selfish. Not one single thing came from the centre of me.

What the hell was that about? At that moment Dinah trotted in and slumped her damp body into her basket at the end of my bed. The room was instantly fragranced with wet dog but I didn't care. I loved my smelly dog and her smelly ways.

"Hah! That's it!" I squealed to myself, sat upright and picked up my pen again. I love my dog. I value my dog. It's as simple as that. A value is something you wouldn't part with if someone tried to take it away from you. Something you keep close to your heart. It could be a thing or a concept or a wild dream but as long as it's yours and you value it, it makes the list.

So I did have values after all.

And they weren't even buried deep in the dark corners of my

soul. No! They *were* things I was certain about and they *were* things I would protect in a hippy-protest-type way. Okay, now for . . .

BELIEFS

So what was the difference? Well, I couldn't very well say *I believe in my dog* or *I believe in my health*, so there must be a difference between the two. I started scribbling again.

VALUE ➔ Something you hold dear,
Hippy protests,
You won't part with it,
You protect it,
Something precious . . .

BELIEF ➔ Something you think is true,
Underpins your actions,
Determines your direction in life,
Beliefs can change . . .

So here I figured out that values tend to remain the same most of the time. I would value my health and my family and my home for a long time to come, but beliefs can change as we change. As we develop and grow. And when they do change, it makes sense that we experience big shifts in energy, emotion and attitude. For example, I had believed that Jack loved me for seven years. Now that belief had changed, I was doing all manner of bizarre things like shutting down my business, swanning off to Turkey and practicing an orangey-yellow meditation in broad daylight.

So I got cracking on my beliefs. I tried really hard to be honest and just write the first things that occurred to me. But it was then, when I was trying to be really very honest with myself, that I realised not all beliefs are good. In fact some are just downright pitiful and can be the root of a person's problems. I actually went through some pain writing down this stuff, but I knew in the faraway parts of my heart, that this was a cathartic thing to do.

I believe...

⚹ That I am generally a good person and I have the right ethics and values.

⚹ That out of the darkest times we can find something good and we can learn about ourselves.

⚹ That travel and experience will nourish and develop my character and help me form a view of the world.

⚹ That I need my friends and family around me to be happy.

⚹ That we should never stop learning.

⚹ That hard work keeps the brain active and helps me to become a strong, ethical person.

⚹ That you reap what you sow. I should treat other people as I would like to be treated.

⚹ That I will never be intelligent enough.

⚹ That I will never look the way I want to look.

⚹ That I will probably always have more love to give than is offered to me.

⚹ That I will never live up to the standards I set myself - they are too high.

And when I looked at all of these beliefs on paper, I felt a teeny bit ashamed. Ashamed because some of them were so pathetic. There was nothing wrong with my life. I was so lucky compared to a lot of people. I had all my limbs, I had my sanity (just), I had a full time job and a family and friends and a great little place to live. Who did I think I was, believing such crap about myself?

Shame on you Jess.

I closed my notebook and flopped backwards onto my bed. I stared at the ceiling.

Jesus Christ, I had a lot of work to do. Fancy believing you will never be intelligent enough. Intelligent enough for who? And just what the fuck is intelligence anyway? And why did I care so much about the way I looked? It's not like anybody was even bloody-well looking. These beliefs were sad. Just plain fucking sad. But at least I'd admitted to them and at least I knew something had to be done.

God knew what, but something had to be done.

A few days later I got up and paced round the office.

It was almost the end of the day and Gillie and I were having a freak-out-type moment about our futures. It was only a few months until our last Firebelly project ended and we had not an inkling of what we were going to do next. "What we need Gillie, is some proper time to think this over. We need some time off."

"Fat chance of that," Gillie replied. "We're busy all summer and then all the school projects start." She started talking about perhaps going away for a weekend. Maybe we could go camping or walking or something like that.

But as she chattered, I knew that I, personally, needed a whole lot more than a weekend. All the thinking I'd done since

I'd met Oliver, and the stillness I'd scratched the edge of when I'd been in Turkey, were things I needed larger measures of. I was thinking in the realms of a couple of weeks. Or maybe even a month.

"A month, Gillie. What about a month?"

She stared at me, jaw dropped, eyes wide. "A month? We can't have a month off work you loon. Firebelly would fall to pieces."

"No it wouldn't, not if we planned it properly. We've only got a couple of workshops booked in for September. We could get someone else to do them for just a few quid. Just think Gillie. A month. A whole month to think this through!"

"But, but... well, where would we go? We're skint remember?"

"I could extend my overdraft."

"Who are you and what have you done with my friend Jess?"

"Shut up! Honestly, I could extend my overdraft, and you can pay me back when you like. We could even go back to Turkey. The last holiday was so cheap, I bet we could get another good deal."

"Jess, don't fucking tempt me. Let's just drop this conversation right now."

"Come on Gillie! I tell you what, I'll call the travel agent now, and if I can't get a month for less than five hundred quid each then I'll forget I ever mentioned it, okay?"

"Five hundred quid? For a month? Impossible."

"Wanna bet?" So I dived for the phone and dialled the number of the company we'd gone through last time. "Hello. I want to book a month's holiday please. To Ipeklikum resort in Turkey. Yes that's right. Flights, transfers and hotel please. Yes. Right. Really? Okay, hang on a second please . . ."

"Well?" Gillie cried.

"Four hundred and eight pounds each, taxes included."

"Oh – my – god. Book it. Bloody, fucking, arsing book it!"

And book it I did.

With a great deal of unexplained, unimagined purpose, I booked it.

WHAT MAGIC WAS THIS?_

I HAD NEVER, ever done anything like this before.

My whole life had been planned down to the last possible second with to-do lists, timetables and bloody cash flow bloody forecasts.

Yet here I was booking a holiday I couldn't afford, deserting a business which was dying on its feet, running my debts up to the max and leaving my life for a whole month. But do you know what?

It felt so right.

For the rest of the summer Gillie and I worked like dogs to get all the business tied up before we left.

We had to manage the cash so that there was still enough in the account to pay our salaries while we were away, and enough to keep things ticking over when we got back. It was tricky but it was possible.

Sometimes I would go off into little trances, searching for a reason to justify my insanity. My conclusion was that this was the only real choice. I didn't really know what I needed the time off for, but I knew it had to happen. To an onlooker, I probably looked fairly capable, more-or-less together, but I knew the inside of me was on the brink of something. Whatever I was on the brink of, I was never going to be pushed into it unless I took myself away from everyday life.

So I was giving myself a big, sturdy shove into the unknown. Shit.

Before I left, I let a few friends know what I was doing. I had an epic phone date with Vicky in which we discussed the general pros and cons of my proposed disappearing and ultimately decided it was a bloody brilliant thing to do. I caught up with my brother on the phone too and whilst we had a lovely chat, he couldn't help slipping in . . . "you will be careful, won't you?", "don't go running off with any slimy Turkish men," and my personal favourite, "just don't go all dippy-hippy-shit on me, okay?".

I even met up with Marcus of all people. I was kind of acting as an intermediary between him and Gillie and I hated to say it but I was actually starting to quite like him. Maybe it was due to the fact that everything was tits-up these days, but since he and Gillie had split I felt able to shed my old problems with him. I had no reason to be suspicious of him anymore, he seemed nothing but pleasant and I have to admit, I admired the way he was handling the break-up. "I still love her Jess, but now I know it's not in the right way. And I respect her for what she did."

When I told Marcus what was going on he practically did a somersault. "God, that's amazing. You're going to bloody love it."

And two days before I left he insisted we meet up for a final pint. I told him not to worry, I would be back, it's not like I was headed for the gallows or anything. But he eyed me over the pint of lager which looked truly massive in his tiny hands and grinned in a very unsettling way. "I don't know Jess. This is your time. A lot can happen in a month."

And with that he presented me with a plain white padded envelope.

"This is just something to keep you busy while you're out there. It'll keep things interesting." Not really knowing how to respond, I took it, squeezed it and felt the vague outline of something small and square. "Ah ah ah," Marcus said, wagging his finger at me, "it is strictly to be packed up and not thought about again until the day you arrive. Understood?"

"Understood." I replied, reluctantly stuffing it into my bag. We chinked drinks, grinned at each other and I wondered how I had come to develop this very bizarre, but very amusing, new friendship.

Gillie, Ella and I had the obligatory girlie nights in and out. Ella was gutted she couldn't come with us but, to be fair, she was busy taking over the world with puppets.

I'd told the girls all about what had happened when I'd bumped into Oliver at the café and they were happy I was finally doing some positive thinking. Then, randomly, Gillie suggested we invite Oliver out for dinner one evening. "He's a nice bloke. We should, you know, acknowledge that or something." So I thought, why the hell not? I certainly owed him dinner after he rescued me with chocolate muffins and meditations.

So we all met up - Gillie, Ella, Oliver and I - in the same café I'd met him in last time. Oliver, as always, was impossibly easy to talk to and poor Gillie and Ella couldn't take their eyes off him. They competed to offer him more wine, more bread, more salad, more salt – anything that might increase their chances of skin-to-skin contact. I couldn't see it myself. Yes, he was impossibly nice but sex appeal just didn't come into it. Oh well, there was no accounting for some people's tastes.

After dinner, Gillie and Ella had consumed so much wine that they went off in search of an off-licence to buy cigarettes. Gillie only ever smoked when she was nervous so I knew something was going on with her. As soon as they were gone, Oliver leaned over the table and said "So come on matey, spill the beans. How's the orangey-yellow world of happiness going?"

I laughed at the fact that he even remembered my little happiness trick.

"Not too bad actually. Not too bad."

"And the notebook?" I rummaged inside my bag and pulled it out to show him that it pretty much came everywhere with me these days.

"Nice one." He said.

"Actually Oliver," I began, "Can I just ask you about something?"

"Fire away." He leaned back in his chair and I got that lovely rush of trust again.

"Well, I was having a little think about everything you said . . . and then I was kind of making some notes about values and beliefs," I blushed a little at the sound of my own voice talking about philosophical stuff so casually. "And, well, I found out that I believe in some pretty shitty things."

"Such as?"

God, this was embarrassing.

I opened my notebook on the pages about beliefs and showed him the ones about my limited intelligence, my crappy looks and my lack of love from other people. "I think these beliefs are terrible. Why did I write them down?"

"Well, you need to think about that," he said.

Was that it? I needed to think about it? Well, I bloody well knew that, didn't I? Then he added "What about if you changed some of the language here? What about if you said, 'I will always live up to my own standards' or 'I will always receive more love than I have to give'?"

"It makes me feel crap Oliver, because there's something inside me that just doesn't believe it."

"So what about your friends and family. Gillie and Ella, for example. Do you feel loved by them?"

"Of course I do! I feel incredibly loved by them."

"So what's the problem?"

"I don't know Oliver, I just don't know." I slumped forward and caught my head in my hands. How very dramatic. And how very wine-fuelled.

"Okay matey." He started slowly. "But if you did know, what would the answer be?"

I burst out, "The answer would be that I am so ridiculously loving. I love people so much and I expect them to love me back in the same way. Why did Jack up and leave? Why is everyone more secure than me? Why can't someone treat me in the ways I always treat them? I'm a really good person . . . I deserve it, don't I?"

And as I listened to my own voice in that weird, disembodied way I was getting very good at these days, I realised something new. I was judging everybody with my own standards. I was expecting from them the same kind of treatment as I was willing to give. It went back to that belief I had about reaping what you sow, treating others as you want to be treated. But that doesn't guarantee you that treatment. For the first time it was dawning on me what a naïve and outdated belief this actually was. You don't always reap what you sow.

And why should you? The world is made up of millions of different personalities, each one with its own set of beliefs, values and behaviour patterns, each one showing love in a different way. It was crazy to expect anything in particular back from them. Why couldn't I just give the love I had to give, in whatever form I fancied and not expect anything back?

Was that possible?

"Of course it's possible Jess. If you make it possible."

Oh bloody hell. My beliefs were morphing in front of my eyes. Helped along by a few glasses of wine and this friendly-faced, spiky-haired man.

I looked towards the door of the café. No sign of Gillie and Ella yet. "So what about this? How the hell do I feel happy for Jack? He's with that bloody Katy now and I want to feel happy for him because if I really loved him I'd be able to do that. Instead I want to break his and her neck." And almost as soon as his name passed my lips, tears clawed at my eyes and my voice cracked painfully. I didn't want to cry here, in this café, at night, before pudding, in full make-up, but it was coming. But Oliver was patient. And so beautifully subtle.

He somehow created a bubble around our table and I was able to cry without being interrupted by well-meaning waitresses. I couldn't believe I was sobbing in front of him. This man I met on a business course. This man who was a travel photographer. This man who my best friend clearly fancied the pants off. But all of those roles faded away as I cried and he was quite simply a man who wanted to help.

He somehow led me from tears to stillness. From stillness to gentle discussion. We talked steadily about how I could move forward from here and I started to feel better. We both agreed that this month away would allow me to focus in on myself and help to strip away some of my Jack-related ties. It would give me space to think.

Space to breathe.

"It's 'you' time matey. Just remember that. You can think more about your beliefs and values and the world of Jess. It's so difficult to do that in everyday life – stepping out of it for a while is a tip-top idea."

"I know, I know, but it bloody well scares the shit out of me!" Oliver smiled in a *that's-my-girl* type way and I knew we were silently agreeing that, in this instance, fear was a good thing.

I'd been absentmindedly flicking through the pages of my notebook whilst I'd been talking and now Oliver leaned forward in interest.

"Can I just pinch a little look Jess?"

"Of course." I said, and slid the notebook towards him. He propped it up on his empty pasta bowl and leafed through it, long, skinny fingers tracing each page as if he could feel as well as read what was there. His face showed absolutely no sign that he thought I was mad / stupid / illiterate so at least that was something.

"This is really interesting," he said. "You've put things in a very clear light."

He'd stopped on a page where I'd been exploring those values of mine. I'd spent quite a bit of time on this, having got a bit mixed up the first time round. And, being the arty-farty type I was, I'd found it much easier to use a mixture of drawings, words and scribbles to describe the things I felt protective of. I mean, over the last few days it had suddenly occurred to me that people generally just accept that say, a house is important, or a job is important, but they don't really – and I mean *really* - think about *why* they're important.

Why do we spend so much time trying to get these things right? Why do we behave in certain ways to get what we think we want? Where are our actions rooted and how are our opinions formed?

I watched Oliver's fingers trace across the page and around the topsy-turvy diagram as he read each section.

So I can live a long & fulfilling life; be **FULL** of energy & vigour.

Health & Fitness

Home

Somewhere to be still; my place; my sanctuary; somewhere to find a sense of self

Freedom

Going where I like, when I like; freedom of thought, expression, action; managing my own time.

Dog

A loyal companion; she gets me outdoors everyday, experiencing fresh air

Independence

Emotional independence; ability to spend time alone & enjoy it; financial independence

My Future?

I want to stay healthy & strong so I can indulge in a FANTASTIC future

Security

Security in myself, my character, who I am & what I do; stillness in my mind

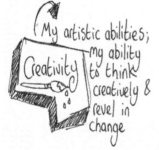

Oliver's finger rested on that last one. I piped up. "It's not that I compare myself to my brother," I said, "It's just that I think so highly of him, I would love to be like him."

"Okay. But you don't compare yourself to him." Oliver looked up and smirked.

"No."

"And do you think your parents are proud of you?"

"Well, I don't know. They never really tell me they are. They're so well travelled, well educated, well rounded. They've been amazing role models for me. I hope they are proud of me."

"I'm sure they are Jess." He closed the notebook, pushed it back towards me and leaned back in his seat. I knew he was ticking something over in his head. "You've just said you don't compare yourself to your brother in the same breath as saying you would love to be like him."

"Oops."

"Well, you could have a think about that. I mean, why give yourself boundaries like that?"

Yet again the man had a point. I had never questioned that underlying thing about living up to standards set by my family. I just thought that was what families were about. You looked up to each other and you got your ideas about life from them. This made my head spin. Where was I supposed to start with that? God, this trip to Turkey was going to be so full of thinking, I wasn't sure I'd even have time for cocktails, sunbathing and swimming. Gillie would not be happy.

"Jess," Oliver said lightly and clicked his fingers up above his head. "Come on. Back to the land of the living!"

"Sorry. I was just thinking about . . . well, never mind. God, Oliver, I think this is part of my problem. Over the last few years I've been so conditioned into planning ahead, organising everything, planning for every eventuality, it seems I am completely incapable of enjoying the here and now. Sometimes I can't even concentrate on what people are saying to me because I'm so busy thinking about the next thing I have to do. It's so bloody rude!"

"Hey matey, chill out. Most people have that problem at least some of the time. But you're right, it's like, crucial to enjoy the here and now 'cos that's really all we've got. And anyway, I've got a couple of little tricks that might help." I picked up my pen, not wanting to miss whatever little gems he was going to pass my way, and I wrote as he talked.

BEING IN THE HERE & NOW!

Rapid Listening → As people talk, repeat their words in your head as quickly as they say them. If you can do this, it's impossible to think about anything else

I gave 'Rapid Listening' a go with Oliver as he talked – he was right, it really worked.

Notice your Senses → Wherever you are, notice how it feels physically to be there. Notice the sights, the smells, the sounds, the textures, the tastes - focus on each one individually

Okay, so I was sitting there in the café at that moment. I noticed how my arm was resting on the edge of a dark, angular wooden table. I noticed the feeling of the smooth wine glass against the palm of my hand and how its rim reflected the cosy, orange glow of the restaurant's wall lights. I noticed the way my legs were crossed and my toes were tapping on the metal table leg. I noticed the rich smell of ground coffee, the sound of the dishes sizzling in the kitchen, the way the waitresses sashayed in and out of the maze of tables, their apron ribbons bobbing behind them.

I noticed it all: the everyday sensations of just being in this place.

Touch, smell, sounds, sights and tastes.

And then I noticed a chilly gust of outdoor freshness, laced with a nicotine edge arriving at our table. It was the girls back from their cigarette quest. "Hello peeps." Ella piped up and slid back into the booth beside me, meaning Gillie could reclaim her place next to Oliver. "You were so bored without us, you actually had to get books out and read!" She quipped, pointing at my notebook.

"Yeah," I replied. "Jeez girls. Never leave me alone with this man again! I was ready to grab the vino and go." I winked at Oliver and he raised his wine glass right above the centre of the table. We all did the same.

"Well in that case, here's to boredom maties!" We all clinked glasses, laughed our little heads off and suddenly it was time for pudding.

At the end of the night, we were bound for the taxi rank in our wonderful drunken splendour, when Oliver pulled me to one side.

"Jess, I almost forgot. I brought you something. Here." He pulled a scruffy, dog-eared paperback book out of his pocket and handed it to me. The Alchemist. By Paulo Coelho. "You could read it while you're away."

"Cheers Oliver."

The book had a quote from Madonna on the front: *A beautiful book about magic, dreams and the treasures we seek elsewhere and then find on our doorstep.* Well, if it was good enough for Madonna, it was good enough for me.

"Just let me know what you think of it," he said, and then quick-stepped up to join Gillie who was several paces ahead. I tucked the book under my arm and smiled at the way he was nudging her playfully in the ribs. Ella hung back to make sure I'd noticed the moment and linked my other arm, pressing me close to her so I could hear her whisper, "Well, well, well, who would've thought it?" I smiled back and we stamped our feet in delight.

Oooh – our Gillie in a new romance. And with a hell of a catch too.

A second later my mobile phone rang. I fished it out of my coat pocket. It was Dad.

"Hi, love. Just checking you're still coming round for dinner tomorrow night so we can see you before you jet off into the sunshine."

"Yep. Certainly am, Dad. Just need to finish a load of stuff at work and then I'll be round, okay?"

"Fine love. And, I just wanted to tell you something too."

"What's up? Is everything alright?"

"Yes, yes, everything's fine. It's just that the strangest thing. I was really taken with the urge to call you."

"Right . . . " This was odd.

"Well . . . I just wanted to tell you that I am so proud of you. Your mam is too. We probably don't tell you enough, but, well, we are so very proud of you love." I stopped walking. Ella stopped too. Dad continued. "The two biggest achievements in my life are you and your brother. I just wanted you to know."

I stood there in the middle of a busy street of pubs and restaurants. People dodging round me. Ella waiting patiently. My phone at my ear. My breath caught in my throat. My heart thumping wildly.

We said our goodbyes and I hung up the phone. What magic was this?

And the question I asked myself over the next couple of days as I wound up my work, packed up my things, locked up the house and arrived at the airport with Gillie, was: how was I going to find more of it?

THE TWO WOMEN stared into the fire in silence.

The flames were calming to a soft ember glow. The warmth of it lulled them into the softness of the night. Jess's last words hung in the air like tiny stars, brand new silver pinpricks drifting quietly along.

"So now I know why you're here Jess. You've been here in Turkey since then?"

"No, no. I did come to Turkey in September. I did come to this resort again. But there's lots more to it than that. The story hasn't really even started yet." Jess stood up and brushed down her upturned jeans.

"Are you hungry? I could do with a snack. And some wine. Yeah, some wine would be good."

Lindy thought wine and snacks sounded perfect, and she was gagging to hear the next part of the story, but was it really a good idea to continue this? Her mum and dad were probably worried by now, and would be furious if she didn't count the New Year in with them. Or would they? She checked her mobile phone.

No messages. No texts. Fuck it.

"Yeah. Wine sounds like a good idea."

"Okay," Said Jess. "You stay here and get this fire going again and I'll get provisions. Give me five minutes."

Jess stretched up to the stars momentarily and then walked off across the sand towards the resort. Right. Get the fire going again. Lindy could do that.

A bit more firewood. A bit more poking with trusty stick.

The story wasn't really anything out of the ordinary.

So Jess was a girl who'd gone through heartbreak and loss. So Jess was a girl who'd changed the direction of her career and therefore her life. Big deal. Who hadn't been through all of the above? Hell, Lindy was slap-bang in the middle of it all and didn't need to be told what it felt like. She was a fucking expert. But she had to admit that there was something about the story that kept her listening.

There were little nuggets of gold sprinkled throughout it that glittered and winked at Lindy so that she just couldn't ignore them.

That borderline hippy-shit about being in the depths of pain and having that soulful, inner voice pipe up and tell you what you really need to do.

All that stuff about choices and taking responsibility for your actions so that you could carve out your own path, even if it did involve untold change.

Keeping a notebook to record and reflect on the good things in everyday life.

Because it was usually there, even if it was peeping out from behind something scary.

All of those things – and the promise of more – kept Lindy on this beach, approaching the dead of night, poking a fire and agreeing to drink wine with a perfect stranger.

For the first time in a long time she trusted her instincts and decided to go with them all the way.

So, she waited. She leaned back into the soft, cool caress of the sand, allowed the warmth of the fire to skim the surface of her skin and she waited for Jess to return.

She waited for the next part of the story.

ACKNOWLEDGMENTS_

This book is the beginning of a story that charts a year of epic transformation for me.

It took years for me to translate that into a novel that maybe, one day, people would want to read. During those years, I was held back by, well, life. You know the kind of thing… falling in love, having babies, battling post-natal depression, living in three different countries, scraping a living, losing loved ones, finding direction. And through it all, there have been a whole tribe of people helping me in more ways than they could know.

It's a daunting thought to imagine writing all of those names down. I am BOUND to miss somebody crucial out as my brain has been plagued by pregnancy hormones several times AND according to my kids I'm too old to remember anything now anyway.

So, I'm going to say a massive thank you to the whole tribe. You know who you are…

The readers, the readers, the readers

The advisers

The encouragers
The inspirers
The lifter-uppers
The texters
The late-night phone-callers
The rejecters
The baby sitters
The feeders
The give-it-a-go editors
The artists
The other authors
The bloggers
The reviewers
The online applauders
The professionals
The non-professionals
The believers
The readers, the readers, the readers

And the names I can pledge to remember (just about) are:

Dad – You're not here anymore but I know you'd be chuffed that I did what I said I was going to do all those years ago. Bloody told you I'd do it.

Mam – Thank you so much for always showing me what a strong, focused woman is and loving me no matter how hippy-shit I get.

Matty – For always being able to make me laugh like nobody else in the world and for never flinching when I described my chick-lit-type ideas.

Baran and Azad – You have always gloriously assumed that I can do this and I know you'll be as excited as me to finally hold this book in your gorgeous little hands.

Mustafa – Basically, there would have been no book

without you, but don't let that go to your head. You are not the husband I planned but you're the one I want with my very soul, and one day, *bir gün*, I know you'll do the washing up.

ABIGAIL YARDIMCI is an author, blogger, and creative mindfulness practitioner. She is a Geordie girl living by the sea in South Devon with her Turkish husband and two terrifying kids. She loves to blog and gets her kicks through mindful parenting styles, creative living and chocolate.

Abigail's writing inspiration comes from scratching the surface of everyday life to find the underlying magic that connects us all. The fire beneath the frustration, the creativity beneath the boredom, the stillness beneath the chaos.

Abigail's debut novel, 'Life Is Yours' is published as the first of a trilogy by BNBS Books and she stays sane in the world of parenting by writing a popular blog called 'Mum In The Moment'. You can find and follow her blog at www.abigailyardimci.com/muminthemoment

Abigail also kinda thrives on social media so join her there to find out more about the Life Is Yours trilogy and loads more:

facebook.com/abigailyardimci

twitter.com/abigailyardimci

instagram.com/mum_in_the_moment

SNEAK PEEK OF 'DESTINY IS
YOURS'_
THE SECOND BOOK BY ABIGAIL YARDIMCI

CHAPTER ONE_
RESPITE

Lindy didn't have to wait for long before Jess returned to their glowing beach alcove, where they'd been sitting for a good while now.

She watched as Jess scuffed through the silvery sand, the sleeves of her purple hoodie rolled up, silver bracelet jangling and blonde waves bobbing around her face. She was clutching an already opened bottle of red wine, two glasses and a paper bag.

"The bloke at the traditional Turkish place opened the bottle for me and said I could have the glasses as long as I return them later. He gave me a proper wink and a nudge but, you know, best to ignore that."

Jess laughed, threw herself down next to the fire and flattened out a plain of damp sand. She planted the base of the glasses firmly and Lindy reached to pour the wine, watching it flow freely into the moonlit glasses, just like the dark, rolling waves only feet away from them. It made that wonderful glug-glug sound of the first pour.

"Thanks Jess. This is so what I need."

"No probs. Turkish wine isn't always up to much but

I've had this one before and it's alright. And wait till you taste this."

Jess unwrapped a small selection of sticky-looking, flaky pastry cakes, all decorated with nuts, seeds and dried fruit and scented with cinnamon.

"Baklava. It's not exactly a bumper bar of Dairy Milk but it'll do."

Jess set the cakes down between them both and Lindy reached for a particularly delicious looking glazed pastry triangle drenched in honey and crushed pistachios. She sank her teeth into it and enjoyed a sudden shot of sweetness that made her shiver. That aromatic honey, pastry as fine as flower petals and a solid, earthy bite to the nuts... she'd never fancied it when her mum had shoved it under her nose before now, but tonight things were different. She could feel it in her bones, in the cool whisper of the breeze.

Tonight there was a new story beginning to unfold for Lindy.

Lindy wondered where her parents would be now. No doubt they'd be shacked up at their favourite dive, taking it in turns to roll their eyes and despair at what they were going to do with their wayward daughter. It was New Year's Eve, after all and they would be expecting her to get in touch before midnight at least. Lindy checked her phone.

There was time yet.

And let's face it, 2006 hadn't exactly been kind to her. She remembered how she'd felt earlier that evening, just before she'd met Jess, when she'd been wandering aimlessly on the beach with only tears for company. She'd felt that familiar sense of dread claw at her and try to pull her so far down so that she might very well become part of the mass of wet sand she was walking on, part of the cold, dark depths of the ocean below. Even here, in the perfectly nice holiday resort her parents had managed to drag her to, away from everything at home that was shit and awful, she hadn't been able to find respite. That was, until she'd spotted Jess's fire in the alcove.

It was as if all of this had been waiting for her. The alcove, the fire, the wine, Jess and her story of heartbreak and pain, magic and hope. She momentarily considered looking around for hidden cameras, for her parents crouching behind a rock with Derren Brown or somebody equally dodgy, only to reveal she'd actually been hypnotised into all of this. But there were no hidden cameras here.

Just some strange coincidence that she was, at last, choosing to embrace.

"Come on then, what happened next? How was the second holiday in Turkey?" Lindy was ready to find out what Jess had done with her huge slice of time back in Turkey. Frittering a whole month away just to ponder the meaning of life seemed like a mental thing to do when you had a failed relationship to mourn, not to mention a flawed business to run. But having heard the reasoning behind it all, Lindy was totally on Jess's side.

Sometimes you just had to say fuck it.

"Well, it was so much more than a holiday that's for certain. Where can I start? I know. Let me tell you about Shit Class Hotel." Jess took an impressive mouthful of wine and wiped her mouth with the cuff of her jumper.

She leaned back into the rock and planted the base of her glass in the sand again, fingers tracing the neck of the glass and her blue eyes alive. Lindy leaned back too and wondered what kind of story could possibly start with a shit class hotel.

CHAPTER TWO_
SHIT CLASS HOTEL

Thanks to our incredibly cheap flight tickets, we arrived at
Bodrum airport at some unearthly hour.

Gillie's gangster-style love interest, Demir, had offered to
pick us up from the airport, having badgered her since our last
holiday with constant texting. When we tumbled out of the
airport into the dry heat of the night, we saw Demir standing
there, in an exact replica of the image we'd joyfully anticipated:
pointy black shoes gleamed to within an inch of their life,
pressed chinos, hair sculpted into a glistening, razor-like point
and a soppy smile on his face that contradicted all of the coiffing
efforts he had made. "Hello girls," he said. "Welcome back my
country."

He air-kissed me on both cheeks and fixed a rushed,
determined kiss straight on Gillie's mouth before whisking us
away in his car.

We drove the couple of hours to Ipeklikum, Gillie in the front
chatting to Demir, and me in the back watching this new world
go by. This really was the first moment I'd had to myself in quite
some time.

Things had been so busy at home what with all the holiday

preparations and sorting out work. Now that I was here, in the back of this bizarre man's car, with the warm wind whipping through the open window and the unfamiliar night landscape whizzing past, I could finally appreciate the weirdness of what I'd done.

There was something comforting about arriving in Ipeklikum. I recognised some of the streets, restaurants and shops as we drove into the resort. *How funny*, I thought, *that a place you've only known for a week in your entire life can coax you back into contentment so very easily*.

Demir stopped outside our home for the month: First Class Hotel. And it looked okay. Maybe not first class exactly, but it looked clean and bright and it would do.

Demir sauntered inside and arranged for the porter to take our bags and show us up to our room. Then he waited obediently in the car as Gillie quite rightly instructed him.

Lacking the natural hospitality of Demir, our porter literally chucked our bags in the corridor leading to our room and shoved the key in my hand saying, "Only one key, okay?"

He then dashed back downstairs to continue watching some Turkish equivalent of Eastenders on the dusty flat screen in reception. Gillie and I were far too excited to be pissed off with him and squeezed ourselves into the little corridor so we could shut the door behind us. Gillie climbed over our haphazardly hurled bags and chirped, "Come on Jess, our room must be just through here... oh."

A world of disappointment was in that 'oh'.

"What is it Gillie?" I asked as I scaled the bags myself and half tripped over to where she was standing. Then I saw it. The corridor that led into our room? It wasn't a corridor. It *was* the room. And gone was the promise of 'two ample-sized single beds' as outlined in the brochure, more like 'one tiny double bed designed for pixies'.

And somehow, though god only knows how, they'd managed to squeeze in a match box sized bedside table, two single red lightbulbs hanging on shoestring wires, and a series of little alcoves built into the wall which we presumed to be the equivalent of a wardrobe.

"Bloody hell, a few days in here and it'll look like an award-winning art installation ."

Gillie slumped down on the bed, knocking her knees on the scarily close facing wall. "Oh but look at this. What do you suppose they were thinking?" Gillie giggled and pointed at the corner of the bed where somebody had quite clearly spent the best part of an afternoon folding every towel, flannel and paper tissue into shapes which resembled perky little swans.

"Hah. You can't have access to basic human rights in this hotel, but you can dry your arse on a towel shaped like a swan!"

Gillie flung herself backwards and laughed up at the ceiling, a mixture of genuine amusement, despair and sleepiness. I then proceeded to give her a running commentary of our new temporary home. "And you will see madam, that if you place one foot, quite literally, in front of the other you can amble down this side of the room to an opening fashioned not with a traditional door, oh no, but with a 1950's synthetic folding mechanism which allows you to access a wonderfully... erm... "

I wedged myself into the bathroom and continued from inside, "a wonderfully condensed bathroom arrangement with the added design feature of sink, shower and toilet all being no more than five centimetres apart. I think you'll find it a very convenient assemblage to rival any other bathroom setting."

I could hear Gillie from the other side of the paper-thin wall. "Stop Jess, you're killing me!".

"But it doesn't stop there. Once you've twisted yourself away from the bathroom's multiple attractions... "

I popped myself out and lurched to the opposite side of the room, "... you'll notice that the room has the obligatory holiday feature of a south-facing balcony. It is disguised behind this rather fetching heavy tweed style curtain. But, if you pull it back... " I heaved the grotesque, dusty curtain with all my might to reveal our last scrap of hope, a balcony with a sea view, "You will reveal this marvellous single French door which opens – wait for it – inwards! So you can bash the well-located bed every time you wish to go outdoors. And you will be no doubt delighted to find that you can actually fit your entire set of toes onto the balcony floor! As for the sea view, if you look hard enough you will discover a chink of rippling ocean can be seen between the two fifteen-story hotels which are not more than fifty yards across the road. It has been known that sunlight can even find its way into this apartment through that very same gap on a completely cloudless day."

I turned round and beamed at Gillie. "Well, I think that concludes the tour of your luxury new dwelling in Shit Class Hotel!"

"Yey for Shit Class Hotel!" Gillie cheered. "Thank you tour guide. Now let's get changed and get out of this place. I want a beer!"

Half an hour later we'd been driven to our old haunt, Beerbelly, and were enjoying a beer, as planned, under the stars.

We'd arrived to find the legendary, long-haired cocktail-maker Mesut and cringey ladies man 'Bad Boy' lounging in a thick cloud of cigarette smoke, watching 'Kill Bill' on the super-sized TV. We flinched a bit when Demir demanded that we be served immediately, especially when the boys protested that it was too late to be serving customers now.

The whole confrontation was delivered in quick, angry

Turkish, but Gillie reckoned Demir had pointed out if Bad Boy could have a scantily clad Essex girl wrapped around him then surely Mesut could be freed up to make a couple of drinks. So Mesut stormed off to the bar, head hung so low that his long black hair blocked out any angry retorts he might be making, and returned seconds later with several bottles of ice cold Efes lager.

Long story short, we were finally here with our beers and the stars. Bad Boy had obligingly disappeared with his clinging Essex girl, Mesut had slumped back in front of his movie, and Demir started to recount the story (though god knows how it turned into an actual story), of our tiny little box room.

"So now," Demir said in fits of giggles. "Jess is calling it 'Shit Class Hotel'! Do you get it Mesut? Shit Class Hotel!" Mesut kept his eyes on the screen but tipped his head slightly and kind of snorted which I assumed was a chuckle, whilst Demir hurled himself back into his chair and bit a cushion to curb his own hysteria.

Gillie and I exchanged glances. Okay, maybe we had to learn a thing or two about the sense of humour over here, because suddenly I had become an award-winning comedian.

And that was the thing, I suppose, that we wanted to get out of this trip. We could become anything we wanted. We could let people think whatever they liked. Nobody knew us, nobody had ties to us, or expectations of us. We could live one long month of blissful, harmonic, euphoric anonymity.

I stretched my legs out onto the table despite a withering glance from Mesut; smiled at Gillie and Demir engaging in an already predictable game of flirtation; leaned back and took a long, cool gulp of beer.

Yup. This was going to be a damn good month.

Printed in Poland
by Amazon Fulfillment
Poland Sp. z o.o., Wrocław